"Michele Perry has captured the message and in her book. It is the message of love. The message of His heart. I pray that as you read this book, your heart will be enlarged and you will become so immersed in Jesus that your eyes are opened to see Him in the lost and broken."

—from the foreword by **Heidi Baker**, PhD,
founding director of Iris Ministries, Inc.

"*Love Has a Face* is an incredible book. Facing her own insurmountable obstacles, Michele was born without her left hip and leg. By the time she was thirteen, she had endured 23 surgeries. In midst of these difficulties, Jesus Himself came to Michele and called her to bring His love to 'the least of these.' Leaving the security of America, Michele has become a one-legged ambassador of love—first to the slums of India and now to the war-torn regions of Southern Sudan. Michele is transforming one of the most dangerous spots on earth, one child at a time, by the loving heart of Jesus. This moving and amazing story will inspire you, too, to be the face of transforming love right where *you* live. We cannot say enough about Michele and her work. You have to read this book!"

—**Wesley and Stacey Campbell**, RevivalNOW Ministries;
Be A Hero (NGO); board members, Iris Ministries

"Michele Perry's book, *Love Has a Face*, is the amazing story of her work with the orphans in Sudan amidst a war-torn populace. It is the inspiring, heart-touching, faith-building story of one of God's greats who, instead of becoming bitter over severe birth defects, has been transformed into a modern-day superhero of the faith. It is not only about the work Michele is doing, but the work one can detect between the lines that God has done and is doing in her—and the importance of the relationship of these two works. I encourage all to read *Love Has a Face*, for in doing so, we will have a better picture of The Face: His face. Michele is the real thing and has written about one of the most important things on the Lord's heart. I hold Michele and her book in high regard and deep respect."

—**Randy Clark**, president and founder, Global Awakening; overseer, Apostolic Network of Global Awakening; founder, Global School of Supernatural Ministry

"Michele Perry makes the timeless request, 'Show me how to love.' In *Love Has a Face*, she shares love stories that come from lessons she has learned. Every story in this book illustrates God's great love for His children. On each page you will see faith, hope and love. Thank you, Michele, for sharing your love story with us."

—**Beni Johnson**, Bethel Church, Redding, California; author, *The Happy Intercessor*

"Michele is a very brave lady who risks her life regularly to bring the love and power of God to the desperate and needy in Southern Sudan. May the Lord give us many more like her! Her mission challenges me to the core."

—**John Arnott**, president, *Catch the Fire, World*

"It has been a joy and privilege to know Michele for all these years and watch what God has accomplished through her. How should I describe her to you? Extraordinary love, courage, commitment, obedience, sacrifice—Michele is a great example of how God can take an ordinary person to accomplish the extraordinary. Her life is an inspiration to all of us! She doesn't allow circumstances to determine her destiny, but pursues God and embraces His love in such a way that it propels her to rise above the problems she faces. This in turn releases God's love, presence, miracles, healing and blessing to the poorest and most destitute in her region of Africa. I trust that by reading Michele's story, you will be challenged to embrace God and His love in such intimacy that you, too, will make a difference in the lives of those you encounter daily. Nothing is impossible for God to accomplish through anyone willing to love the way He loves and to obey Him in anything He calls you to do in life."

—**Mel Tari**, author, *Like a Mighty Wind*

"When we commend a book, we are also commending the author in character, integrity and ability as a writer. But I wish to go even further. I am commending to you the very fingerprints of God upon Michele's life and the flow of God in, on and through her. Michele is a remarkably capable author who expresses herself with incisive, engaging skill, weaving life into the stories she tells in a way that invites you not only into her story but into the life behind the story. More than that, Michele herself is a story, written by God's hand, infused with God's light, pulsating with God's love and radiant with God's joy and power. I commend to you my friend Michele, whose heart will capture yours as you read this book."

—**Dr. Tom Wymore**, simple/house church coach,
The International Church of the Foursquare Gospel

"Perry's tender story may very well change your life. Embrace every word!"

—**Beverly Lewis**, New York Times bestselling author

LOVE HAS A FACE

LOVE HAS A FACE

Mascara, a Machete and One Woman's
Miraculous Journey with Jesus in Sudan

MICHELE PERRY

FOREWORD BY HEIDI BAKER

Chosen

a division of Baker Publishing Group
Grand Rapids, Michigan

© 2009 by Michele Perry

Published by Chosen Books
A division of Baker Publishing Group
P.O. Box 6287, Grand Rapids, MI 49516-6287
www.chosenbooks.com

Printed in the United States of America

Library of Congress Cataloging-in-Publication Data
Perry, Michele, 1977–
    Love has a face : mascara, a machete, and one woman's miraculous journey with Jesus in Sudan / Michele Perry ; foreword by Heidi Baker.
      p. cm.
    ISBN 978-0-8007-9478-1 (pbk.)
    1. Perry, Michele, 1977– 2. Missionaries—Sudan—Biography. I. Title.
BV3625.S83P47 2009
266.0092—dc22   2009013484

10   11   12   13   14   15   16   8   7   6   5   4   3

For the children of Sudan
and all those who dare to embrace
the unpaved road into God's heart.

Contents

Foreword

I often get asked these questions: What is the key to revival? What is the secret that enabled you to plant thousands of churches in just a few years in one of the poorest nations on earth? What is your five-, ten-, twenty-year church-planting strategy?

My answer is simple. My answer is always the same. First, we are called to love God powerfully, deeply and intensely. And second, we are called to love our neighbors in the same way. The plan never changes. The strategy remains the same. This kind of fruitfulness can flow only from a place of radical intimacy.

I believe that revival does have a face. It does look like something. It looks like love. It looks like stopping daily for the one in front of you and looking into his or her eyes. You have to see the one. If you cannot see the one, you will not be able to deal with the multitudes. If you see the one, you will understand suffering, because you will see one dying child under a bridge. You will see one baby with AIDS. You will see one widow living alone under a tree. Revival is about looking into his or her eyes and seeing Jesus look back at you.

Michele Perry has captured this message of revival in her life and in her book. It is the message of love. The message of His heart.

For many years I have seen visions of a radical army of laid-down lovers—a whole generation of those who are so full of passion and intimacy that they run into the darkness without fear to bring in the lost bride. Michele is a forerunner of this new breed of lovers, those who live only to pursue a passionate love affair with Jesus. They are so full of the Presence that no matter what they are asked to do, they say yes. There is no "no" left in them.

While reading this book, I found many of my own words echoing back to me. It is clear that Michele carries the very heart and DNA of Iris Ministries. It is a privilege and honor to have Michele as part of our Iris family.

I pray that as you read this book, your heart will be enlarged and you will become so immersed in Jesus that your eyes are opened to see Him in the lost and broken. I pray that you will be stripped of the complications and concerns that cause you not to see clearly, so that you will no longer be able to pass by without stopping for the one in front of you. I pray that as you yield to His immeasurable, ceaseless, bottomless love, you will soar on the wings of passion and compassion, pouring out the wine and oil of the Holy Spirit over your nation.

Heidi Baker, PhD
Founding director, Iris Ministries, Inc.

Acknowledgments

Thank you to all of my family in Jesus who have traveled this journey with me into His heart of love. Thank you to the ones who have laughed and cried and stood with me, believing for morning at midnight. Thank you to my friends who have called forth my deepest desires, my most audacious dreams and even the longings I once was afraid to embrace.

Mary-Pat and Bill, thank you for being there and being family. Heidi and Rolland, thank you for loving me, believing in us and cheering us on. Mom and Dad, thank you for being you and giving me wings. I love you! Mel, thank you for watching out for me and telling me to go for it!

Thank you to my friends new and old who have loved us and prayed, and to those from whom I have learned along the way: Tom, Mike and Chris, Deborah, Randy, Janet and Jimmy, Chris J., Hope, Sandi, Briskilla, Julie, Pamela and Tony, Steve, Brian and Candice, Denise, Georgian and Winnie, Jennie-Joy, Pam, Elizabeth, Lissa, Paul, Bill and Beni, Danny, Gordon,

Darrel, Abe and Lil, Lesley-Anne, Charles and Anne, Katherine, Mark B., Felicity and Tony, Annalisa, Antoinette and their family.

To those who have prayed, helped and made this book a reality: Jane, this journey would not have been what it has without you. I have learned so much—thank you! Claire, thank you for the much-needed commas and encouragement. My new family with Chosen, it has been an honor and privilege to travel these miles and pages together.

And most of all I want to thank my beautiful Jesus, who captured my heart so long ago and is the reason I even have a story to tell.

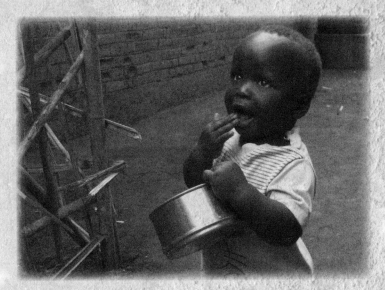

Baby Immanuel, our daily reminder that "God is with us"

1 _Stepping Downward_

I woke to the sound of frustrated voices outside my window speaking in muted tones of Kawkwa and Juba Arabic. It was not yet 7:00 A.M.

What now? We had been open only a few weeks. Every day seemed to bring more challenges than answers to solve them. What had God gotten me into?

I threw on a long skirt and stepped outside into the early morning light to find out what the problem was. Several of our older children were looking at a hole in the back wall of our rented building. Though not large, the hole served as clear evidence that our bricks had been chipped away by AK-47 rounds during the night. And one-quarter of the back of our bamboo fence had grown legs and walked off with the neighboring community. One of our younger boys brought rocks to me that had been thrown at our windows. We were getting quite the reception.

I looked back at our small courtyard to the thirty or so people who were already waiting to see me. The gunfire had kept me up most of the night, and our three youngest had managed to take up the remaining hours before dawn. I had not even had time to wash my face. And I am not a morning person.

What was I going to do? Jumping on the next flight back to the States to pursue a career as a coffee-shop barista definitely crossed my mind. But my thoughts were quickly distracted by a small tug on my skirt.

"Mama, *garhol*." ("Mama, my throat hurts.") I looked down into two intent, dark eyes asking me to make it all better. Barista-hood would have to wait. Another day of motherhood in Sudan had begun.

Life in a Fishbowl

I love my life. I really do. I love it so much that I want to share it with you. Let me begin by greeting you, for greetings are important in Sudanese culture.

You are most welcome! Welcome to a glimpse of life here: its joys, its challenges, its heartaches and its triumphs. Welcome to where I live—a place called Yei in the far recesses of the bush of southern Sudan, along the borders of the Democratic Republic of Congo and Uganda. It is the last place I ever expected to find myself.

I am a city girl at heart. I have always loathed camping and have never been too fond of dirt. I like perfume, mascara and Starbucks coffee. I love the ocean. I grew up in Florida, so swimming is part of my DNA. I really enjoy running water and electricity. I do. So how is it that a little beach-loving Floridian city gal wound up in the landlocked African bush with none of the above? And how is it that she has never been happier? (Okay, I bring the perfume, mascara and coffee with me—that helps.)

How could I be happy in a place so far removed from all I have ever known? I invite you to venture farther into one of my days to find out. The particular day I have begun to describe to you dawned with scenarios that were often repeated during my first months in Sudan.

After waking to the aforementioned morning reception, I spent the next three hours finding out if we had enough beans for lunch, sorting out household chores and meeting with each little group waiting to see me. It was 11:00 before I had the chance to drink my cup of coffee or wash my face.

I soon noticed a slight man sitting off to the side snoozing in the shade of our building. I went over and introduced myself. He looked up at me with a big, toothless grin. He had heard about our problems last night. We had had a break-in the night before, right? (Yes, we had discovered a few things missing beyond the bamboo fencing, but we had not told anyone . . . hmm. And it was amazing; he knew just what they were.) Would we like to hire his services as a guard? he asked.

I was not sure whether to laugh, cry or tell him off. It did not even occur to me to call the police, as there were not any. Our mystery was solved. The clairvoyant culprit was sitting in front of me asking for employment. We did not know what else might happen that would require his protective services, he informed me. I had flashbacks to 1980s mafia movies.

Taking his résumé, I thanked the man for his time and told him I would pray about his offer. If I was not learning anything else here in Sudan, I was learning to talk to God before doing anything—to find out His take on it, because He is always right and knows way more than I do!

I went over and began greeting the remaining 26 people waiting to talk to me. All were there to give me children. This scene was repeated every day for three months. Every morning and every evening for three months. What do you do in the face of such need?

I listened to each person's story:

"My sister died, and I cannot afford to take in her children."

"My husband left me, and my new husband does not want my children."

"I cannot afford school fees. I cannot afford food."

Every story was unique. Every story was the same. I did not know what to do. How could I? I was still learning how to introduce myself in the language. I was still learning how to talk. My two-year-olds had more vocabulary than I did. Perhaps they should decide who got to live with us. Yet I was learning, I was learning, to look through eyes of love and express God's heart to the ones around me.

One by one, I talked with and cried with and listened to each person God had brought to us. I knew they were not there by accident. *I may not be able to meet all their needs*, I thought, *but I can at least give them the dignity of caring enough to listen and pray with them about what is on their hearts.*

Finally all the stories had been shared and the decisions offered. Seven more children were put on our growing waiting list; two were moving in with us right away, and five would study in our school when it started.

I took my notes and walked back to my room. I looked down at my arms. I knew I was no way near that tan. The Sudanese dirt had been ground into my sweat-drenched skin, two babies had already peed on me and it was not yet lunchtime. I could hear more people just arriving as greetings were exchanged and my name was mentioned. I decided I would try to sneak past them to grab a quick bath. Talking to a clean missionary had to be better than talking to a dirty one.

How I thought that would work I do not know. I stick out just a little bit here.

I grabbed my bucket and headed to the bathing room. Too late. I was seen. No supernatural intervention rendered me unnoticed. So I waved in greeting on my way. It is rude here to not extend any form of greeting.

If I had been Sudanese no one would have cast a second glance. But I am very white, and everyone was fascinated. In addition, I have one leg and walk with crutches, making my white appearance all the more fascinating. Privacy here is indeed a relative concept, and the whole world knows when I take a bath in Sudan. It is life in a fishbowl.

I was beginning to think we did need a guard—not so much to fend off nocturnal intruders, but to seat people somewhere on the other side of our small compound so I could get to the bathing area and take a bath without an audience. Every time I stepped out of my room for those first twelve weeks, a crowd was waiting in the small outer courtyard that separated my door from the bathing rooms.

When I say "bath," don't envision anything too fancy. We do not have bathtubs or hot showers. We do not even have running water. These bathing areas are simple concrete slab structures with tin doors that are falling off rusted hinges. A makeshift drain drains the water, unless one of the children's shirts gets wadded in the way. You carry with you your bucket of water, a cup to pour the water over yourself, soap and a towel.

Furthermore, the building we rented in our early days was a bombed-out, bullet-riddled shell that survived the war years. Our doors and windows had bullet holes in them, many right about eye level if you were under ten years old or four feet tall.

Being the incredibly astute missionary that I am, it had taken me only five months to realize that the perforations lacing our walls were made by machine gun ammunition. I had just thought it was odd that they would make doors with holes in them. A cultural innovation? An adaptation for increased ventilation? It took some Western visitors to point out the truth to me.

It occurred to me that our bathing room doors had bullet holes in them, too. I hoped no one was that curious.

I took my bucket, hung my towel over the door for a little more privacy and washed as quickly as possible. Relaxing, leisurely bathing rituals were a dream from another lifetime. I emerged from the bathing area to an audience of waiting onlookers. They all clapped and cheered when they saw me. Little did I know that my entrance was a command performance. I did not know whether to bow, give an encore or imitate a tomato (in color at least).

The bell rang for lunch. I did not need to ask what was on the menu. It was the same every day in those days: beans and boiled maize flour called *posho* cooked in large pots over a charcoal fire. Dinner was usually a repeat performance of lunch with some small variations.

I had been eating beans every day without a break for well over six months since arriving in Africa. I just could not eat any more beans right then. I decided fasting lunch was a great option. I snuck out the side entrance of our building and the side gate of our compound to go check my email before attending to the waiting crowd.

What Are You Doing?

For five minutes I was clean. That was something to revel in, especially as it was dry season and the hottest time of year where I lived—the season when many of the foreigners prefer to leave town for cooler climates. In Yei we do not have summer and winter, hot and cold. We have wet and dry, hot and hotter. As I walked, large four-ton trucks whisked past me in clouds of dust that stuck to the rivulets of sweat running down my face. So much for clean. It was nice while it lasted.

As the U.N. convoys swept past me and I traversed the red dirt mountain range generously called a road, my heart began to wonder: *What does home look like, Jesus? Is it really a building made of bricks that is one bombing away from oblivion?* Surrounded by bombed-out skeletons of once-grand structures, I had been thinking on that a lot since arriving here.

What really matters if your world can be blown apart in an instant? What does love look like to those who have had their dreams shredded by decades of the ravages of war? What remains that is safe to trust in? My mind wandered as I picked my way through canyons and valleys in the road.

It took me fifteen minutes of walking along that dusty red road to get to the converted shack that housed my connection with the outside world, but it should have taken only half that long. I was in no hurry. I took my time to take in the setting around me. I still had the feeling that I was walking through an issue of *National Geographic*. They really do live in mud huts with grass roofs here. It is not trick photography. Sometimes it felt surreal.

I like to soak things in. And I like to meet people. I like to look in their eyes and show them they are worth seeing, worth stopping for. Jesus stopped for me; I want to stop for them. As I walked, one petite elderly woman in a fitted, blue floral print dress came toward me. Her scarf-covered head was bowed as she shuffled along the uneven road. She got to me and stopped. I stopped, too, and extended my hand in the customary greeting: right hand extended with the left placed on your forearm and a slight bow to show honor to the one you are meeting.

"How are you?" I asked in my broken Arabic.

"I am sick," she replied, slightly taken aback at the little white woman with one leg and crutches trying to speak Arabic to her.

"Where is the problem?" I asked.

She pointed to her back and stomach and said she had "fever." I asked her if I could pray with her for healing. This was more important than my waiting emails. She agreed, and we prayed a simple prayer.

The prayer was not long. It was not complicated. It was the simplicity of a child asking a loving parent for help. She never closed her eyes or bowed her head. She stared at me the whole time I prayed. How do I know? I stared back. Open-eyed prayer. Her expression never changed. She gave no indication that anything happened at all.

I asked her, "Mama, how are you now?"

"I am fine," she said. "The pain has left." No *Thank You, Jesus*, no emotion, no hint of any difference in her at all, except that her shuffle became a full-blown step. She and I walked away in opposite directions.

What was that about? I wondered. No answer came.

Once at the shack, my Internet session was beyond frustrating. Its connection speed made dial-up look state-of-the-art. In two hours I downloaded and sent as many emails. I was hot, dusty, tired and completely unable to accomplish even a fraction of the work that was pressing on me.

There were no miraculous letters in my inbox. No one had pledged two hundred thousand dollars to meet our immediate needs. No one had bequeathed to us his great-grandmother's million-dollar estate. In fact, I did not have news of any monies coming in. The joy of seeing a woman healed on the way to the shack was eclipsed by the looming reality of budgets and necessities with no visible way to meet them.

I felt the weight of it all pushing down on me. And there were at least twenty more people seeking help who were waiting for me to return. I felt heavy. I walked home in the afternoon heat. It was about three o'clock.

What are You doing, sweet Jesus? What are You doing? Are You really here? I just need to know You are here. My prayer went unvoiced, but not unheard.

Baby Ima

I arrived home to our familiar bamboo fence and took a deep breath in preparation for meeting with those waiting for me. To my surprise, for the first time since we had opened our doors on Christmas Day, the crowd had dwindled. I was left with one lone visitor.

He was a slim man of middle age. His shoulders sagged under an unseen weight. He looked heavier than I felt. I walked over to him and introduced myself. He went on to tell me that his daughter had died in childbirth a few weeks back. She had given birth to a small son. With the mother gone, his family had no way to feed the baby.

It was a story that has repeated itself countless times in these parts. According to some, southern Sudan is the second most expensive place in the world. Yes, you read the words correctly. It is second to Tokyo. In the southern Sudanese capital of Juba, a small mud hut worthy of being condemned can go for as much as two thousand U.S. dollars a month. And it costs well over a hundred dollars a month to feed an infant on formula. The average salary, if a person is fortunate enough to have one at all, is about half that.

The grandfather told me that this baby, not yet two weeks old, had been fed on cornmeal and water. The options were obvious. If we did not take this little one, he would certainly die. I told the man to bring me the baby so we could see him. I knew how dangerous this would be. He was my first baby. I knew that as soon as I laid eyes on him, there would be no letting him go, no matter how expensive he was.

As the man left our compound to retrieve the baby, I asked God, "What is the baby's name?" Immediately the reply came: *His name is Immanuel.* I thought God was being figurative and was trying to give me encouragement that He was with us, as *Immanuel* means "God with us."

A short while later the man returned with a small bundle in his arms. I looked at this tiny form almost completely hidden by the four layers of fabric wrapped around him. I asked what the baby's name was. "His name is Immanuel," the man said.

I could scarcely believe my ears. *God, are You really here?* I had asked. My silent prayer had been answered in a baby named Immanuel. Tears began to build in my eyes. With wonder I took him in my arms, peering into the sleeping face of God's answer to my question, and thus baby Ima became our smallest family member yet.

He was frail and sickly, but he was a fighter. He survived all the faltering attempts of someone who knew nothing about babies. He lived through a measles outbreak and a cholera epidemic. He made it through growing up his first year in a large family. Now he is a downright fat toddler. Every day he toddles around on his chubby legs with a huge grin that continually reminds us, God is indeed with us.

It was a message I desperately needed to hear the day he came. I was clear across the planet from my family and loved ones in a completely foreign culture. Nothing was even vaguely familiar. People were shooting machine guns at night right behind us. Our water supply was a hand pump that the community would let us access only in the middle of the night.

I did not come on a scouting mission. I did not do a feasibility study. God said go. I went. I really had very little idea of what He was getting me into. And once I was in the middle of it, I needed to be reminded that He really did know where Yei was, even if most of the world did not.

So Jesus sent us Ima to let me know that He knew where we lived. And He was intent on living with us.

Fried Green Termites

Dinnertime came that night with a surprise.

Toward the end of dry season the flying ants come out in force. You might call them the biggest termites you have ever seen. They swarm the lights in early evening. They get into everything. One night a visitor even awoke to her floor moving—they had swarmed under the door to blanket her room. I am not talking about three or four, or even thirty or forty. I am talking about bugs of biblical proportions.

Well, this city girl does not do bugs. Not crickets or spiders or ants or wasps or roaches or flying termites. Not a one. But in this season, they are inescapable, in more ways than one. And termites, I came to discover, are a dinnertime delicacy. The southern United States is known for fried green tomatoes. We in southern Sudan pride ourselves on our fried green termites.

That's right. They get fried, stewed, boiled and baked into every concoction you would never want to imagine. And my children were all on the edge of their seats to see how Sudanese their little white mama really was.

I vaguely recalled the table being laden that morning with small insects drying in the sunshine, their wings meticulously broken off one by one. I honestly thought my younger boys were simply bored. Little did I know that these insects were on their way to my dinner plate that evening.

The whole compound grew still. I felt all eyes follow the plate that was brought to me. As my dinner was unveiled, I laid eyes on the glistening brown, oil-laden fried shells of the bugs that had flown around our compound the night before. You could have heard a pin drop. Everyone was holding his or her breath in anticipation of my reaction.

A million dietary excuses and sanitary objections flooded my mind in the space of less than ten seconds. "Wow," I heard escape from my lips. I mean, what else can you say in the face of bugs for dinner? Wow.

When in Sudan in termite season, I thought, *eat termites*. I delicately took my spoon and scooped a few fried pieces onto it. *It is only protein, Perry. You are a Sudanese in training now. It is a mental thing. Get over it.* Tentatively I put the spoon into my mouth and began to chew the crunchy contents.

It tasted buttery and a little salty—not too unlike burnt popcorn. It was not that bad. I took another bite with more confidence. *Hey, I can do this.* I looked at my kids and gave them a thumbs-up and a smile. "Mmmmm, *kweis, kweis*" ("very good").

The shout of triumph could have been heard in Khartoum! They cheered and cheered. "Mama, you are a real Sudanese now! If you stay here long enough, your skin will even become nice and black like ours." I had no doubt of the truth of that statement. But not for the reasons they might think.

What does it take to be Sudanese? It is not as hard as I had supposed. It takes only a heart to love and learn, a commitment to be real and a willingness to try termites.

Jerry-Can Litanies

It had been a long day. I was tired, to say the least. But I was not about to miss my favorite part of daily life here. And I had just conquered a dinner that might make even a tough guy think twice. It was cause for celebration.

Every evening our kids break out the plastic jerry cans, pot lids and bamboo sticks and go to town. They sing and dance their hearts out to Jesus. Orchestrated chaos might be an accurate description. Our highly skilled percussion section of ten- to twelve-year-old children pounds out rhythms of God's heartbeat under our little bit of African sky. It is truly a family affair, with everyone joining in, from the youngest to the oldest. While rhythms of worship fill the night, some of our children are singing, most are dancing, but all are a part of this jerry-can litany of praise to our King.

I cannot imagine anything more pleasing to God's heart. I bet He silences the angels to hear true worship rise from this war-torn patch of earth. All the frustrations of the day faded into the night as I heard little voices crying out to the One who is altogether lovely and faithful. In the middle of holy dust and ear-jarring cadences, I knew there was no place I would rather be.

They introduced a new song that night. This one was in English: "I will never leave my Lord till I die, till I die. I will never leave my Lord till I die."

These who had seen mortars drop and lost loved ones to the violence of conflict knew all too well the reality of the words they were offering in worship. Two-year-old Viola climbed into my lap and snuggled her head into my arms. Mama's lap is a great place to fall into the land of dreams. I felt tears silently begin to wet my face.

It was almost too much. At moments like this I wondered if I would wake up back in America and discover that this was a dream or vision.

Was this really real? Did I really have thirty-plus children calling me Mama in the middle of Sudan? Did a woman just get healed on the way to the Internet? Did we just take in our first infant? Was I really holding my promises from heaven in my lap and looking into their eyes every day?

As I watched my growing entourage of children and toddlers jumping and dancing in the moonlight, I realized that I hardly felt qualified for the next stage of my journey. What would it mean to love little Viola, who was curled up in my lap, into her destiny? Holding her when she was two was one thing, but what would love mean when she was ten and twenty?

The dust cloud ascended like incense before His throne. The jerry cans slowed to a meditative beat, and the singing became soft. One by one the children knelt down with their faces in the dirt, or they stood there with their hands lifted to their King.

Was this what revival looked like? I did not know. That was for history to decide, not us. But I did know, in that moment, that I was watching His Kingdom come and His will be done, if only for an instant, on earth as it is in heaven. And that was all that mattered.

The sun set on our prayers. The children lay down on their mattresses, and we tucked them in. We would not have beds for a few more months. As I looked at their sleeping faces illumined by the faint glow from a kerosene lantern, I again wondered about the days ahead. Instability loomed on the horizon.

But, termites aside, it was not such an abnormal day. It was a day of learning how to love and how to see people as God sees them.

Jesus, Teach Me How to Love

There is a pace to life in the bush. It can be demanding in its intensity and infuriatingly slow all at the same time. Life here is a constant paradox that invokes questions and compels an inner journey. New life grows up in old ruins. Development thrives right alongside destruction.

I have been writing these pages from the semi-dark of another evening with no electricity on the waning recesses of my laptop battery. My "shower" is sitting in the plastic jerry can about ten feet away. I think a mouse just danced over my foot. My arms look tanner than yesterday, but I know it will all wash off.

I am no super saint. And I am certainly no suffering missionary. There are moments a hot shower would be lovely, but it cannot compare to being in the middle of God's dreams.

How did I wind up here doing this? I began a journey. I said yes to a downward trail of humility to find His heart, to find what is really real. I prayed a dangerous prayer a little over a decade ago: *Jesus, teach me how to love.*

Many of you have picked up this book thinking it was about Sudan. It is. But what my current address reads is the secondary story. I would not be living where I do if I had not stepped off the paved road in search of what it means to love and be loved. All journeys that really matter start deep inside us. This one did for certain.

I invite you to spend a few hours in our world here with me. Come experience life in a recovering war-torn African nation. Encounter the paradox and embrace the journey. Celebrate the simplicity of the Gospel as miracles happen in the mud. Recapture the eyes of a child, take a deep breath and start to play with angels. Learn to see hidden treasures caught up in worthless existences.

Most of all, I invite you into my journey of discovering more about what it means to live loved by God and to become an expression of His love to the people around me. No matter where in the world we reside, it is this journey into God's heart that will lead us home.

That is where we are going. Life does not always lend itself to roadmaps. But they make most of us more comfortable. I want you to keep reading—right to the edge of the map. And then step off the known path into your own story lived from the center of His heart.

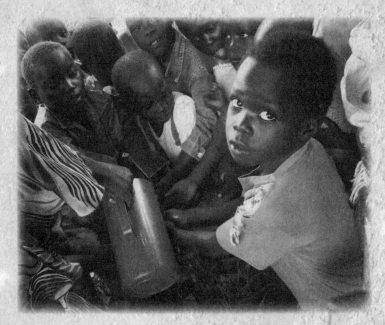

When love looks like a drink of water

2 Love Has a Face

The light filters in my window through a cloud of dust raised by little feet running past. Giggles and squeals punctuate the afternoon heat. We have just finished our noonday meal. Once again it was beans and posho, the boiled maize flour that fools many a visitor into expecting mashed potatoes—until they taste it.

I am sneaking a few moments of quiet in my room. Only ten by twelve feet, it is not a big room. It is just enough for my bed, desk, wardrobe and a table where I keep a small kerosene fire hazard for heating water for my coffee. It has a crumbling cement floor, a folding chair and a bullet-riddled door that barely closes. My prized possessions are the plastic Rubbermaid containers I man-handled over two continents to get here. They are the only things the rats have not eaten through. Peeling, painted white cement walls, a few small knick-knacks and the ever-present layer of red dust complete the ensemble.

It is not much. But in the year and a half I have called it home, it has become strangely familiar. The early mornings are my favorite times, as the light dances in my window and lands in a lovely puddle on my bed. For about an hour, the dinginess of my little room is overtaken by beautiful rays of sunshine. No, it is not much. But I miss it when I am gone. I never thought a dilapidated building with no privacy whatsoever would make it onto my list of favorite places to be.

For much of my life I have been on a search for identity, a quest for belonging, a treasure hunt for greatness. In one word, I have been looking for a place my heart could call "home." But I did not find these things where I expected to find them. I did not realize that what I was looking for would be found in one very unexpected place. And it had nothing to do with a physical address or a successful résumé.

Love Is His Meaning

Even as a child, I was a bit of a romantic. I do not mean a mushy sort of romantic, but as a little girl my heart cried out for more than I could see. It longed for a love bigger than I was and more powerful than my fears. One night I met Him.

I was seven. I did not know what theology was. All I knew was that I was scared. I was facing a serious spinal surgery and had overheard that I could die. I did not know what that meant really. But I knew it was final. And I did not know what would happen next.

I was no stranger to the world of hospitals and doctors. I was born missing my left hip, leg and kidney. I had a plethora of birth defects that required 23 surgeries by the time I was thirteen. I used crutches to walk (and still do). But I was never as scared as I was that night.

I could barely breathe. What would happen if I died or woke up confined in a body that could no longer move? All I had was a cry: "Jesus, if You are who those stories in that book say You are, then I want to know You!" Instantly, supernaturally, normally—as if it had happened a million times before—He was there.

I will never forget that moment. Stories I had read came alive in the person standing before me. He was no fairy tale or imaginary mirage from a land called Pretend. He was real. The Man who walked on water walked into my bedroom. It was that simple.

The love in His gaze made time stand still. My heart cried over and over again, "You are real! You are real. Of course, You are real." It made all the sense in the world to me.

There He was, in my room. He looked with eyes that saw deep inside of me and loved every part. The good parts, the not-so-good parts, the pretty parts, the broken parts—He loved them all! And the minute He appeared, fear left so quickly that the memory of it vanished as well.

As I tell you about my encounter with Jesus, the memory is so vivid that it seems as though it happened only twenty minutes ago, rather than twenty years. I looked into His eyes of liquid love and got lost. Was it ten seconds? Was it ten hours? It did not matter. All of eternity was found in His eyes.

What color were they? In His eyes every color possible was perfectly placed in mosaic irises that poured out grace, mercy and truth. His eyes were the color of laughter. They were the colors of love, compassion, kindness and the strength of steel.

I looked into the face of Love. Fierce gentleness, radical grace and dangerous tenderness surrounded me as His gaze wrapped itself around my heart. I could never go back. My life started over that night. I could have looked into His eyes forever and never moved.

He spoke, and the wheels of destiny and time began spinning on a journey that has led me to where I am now. He told me that if I followed Him I would see whole groups of people in other places in the world come to know Him.

"When do we leave, Jesus?" He just smiled. Waterfalls of joy collided with the songs that echo and resound in the canyons of forever, and they all spilled out together as He laughed.

I looked in His eyes and knew. Love was His meaning. I did not have the words then. It has taken years to find them. But once you have seen His eyes, you know. Love is His meaning. It belongs to no other.

He is the definition of love. He is its substance, its beginning and its end. Love that is true and real looks like what I saw in His eyes.

I met the Man who walked on water. He chased away my fear as a little girl. I had that surgery. I recovered. I grew. I learned. My life started that night. And so did my journey to find His heart.

My Love Is Too Small

I grew up in north Florida and left at seventeen years old for university. By the time I went to college, not only did I have a medical history longer than that of most people I know combined, but I also had a list of accomplishments that could rival those of many twice my age.

I became a professional motivational speaker at the age of nine. At ten I lobbied malpractice reform and met with government officials. By sixteen I conducted leadership development training, did consulting work and was publishing articles. I had intricate ten-year plans for global takeover. I had it all together. I was a professional. I was known. I was a success. So I thought.

My freshmen dorm at Baylor University in Waco, Texas, was right across the street from a gathering called "Church Under the Bridge." It met open-air under the I-35 overpass at Fourth and Fifth streets. On one of my first Sundays at school I heard their music playing. Curious about the crowd I saw, I decided to check it out.

I was a suburban, middle-class white girl, an only child, who had never really seen a homeless person up close and personal, let alone talked with one. They were the people who caused us to roll up our windows as we passed them, checking our car locks and carefully averting our focus to the parked traffic so as not to make eye contact.

I made my way across four lanes of traffic to the large underpass island where the music was emanating. There was no building. The stained glass and padded pews of my former experience were nowhere to be found. I was surrounded by towering concrete pillars, folding chairs and worship sounds punctuated by car horns and traffic noise from the interstate above my head.

My eyes surveyed the crowd. The hair on the back of my neck was beginning to stand at attention. One group of rather forbidding-looking people with black leather and spiked hair stood in the corner. The homeless were milling through the area. To my left sat several ladies who obviously worked the streets. I let out the breath I had unconsciously been holding when I recognized a few faces from freshmen orientation. I scanned the gathering and spotted one or two professors. It could not be *that* dangerous. Professors were there.

A petite woman with light brown hair stepped up to the microphone and began leading us in worship songs that sent chills down my spine. I looked at the gray gravel beneath my feet, up to the freeway above my head and over to the children running through the place laughing. Somehow it just seemed right. *I bet Jesus would like it here*, I thought. *I bet He would feel at home.*

I found an unoccupied, flimsy folding chair. It was brown and had initials carved into it. I started to sing along and feel marginally at ease. Before long, two men came and sat on either side of me. They reeked of alcohol and had not had a bath in a long while. Their eyes were bloodshot and glassy. One looked at me. I tried not to notice. I closed my eyes and tried to focus on the music or look spiritual or something. The other whipped out a pack of cigarettes and began to impersonate a chimney.

It was not long before I was missing the recesses of my choir loft and folder. Stained glass was looking pretty good. Jesus may have been comfortable under the bridge, but I sure was not. I do not remember what was preached that day. But I will never forget what I learned.

As soon as it was polite to do so, I tried to slip away unnoticed back to my dorm. I was relieved the experience was over. It reminded me of a time during high school when I was on vacation with my mom in Seattle and we wound up walking down the wrong street. Addicts were shooting up heroine, and prostitutes were selling their wares. I was so scared that I hid in the hotel room for the next two days.

As I made my way back toward my dorm, I realized I had two escorts. The guys sitting beside me were now walking with me. I had a small entourage. My heart was pounding. Every *Law and Order* episode I had ever seen flashed through my head at once. But I did not want to be rude or show I was flustered. That would not be nice. And while I was not trained in many things, I had definitely been trained to be nice at all costs. Isn't that what Jesus would do?

They stopped at the intersection when they saw I was safely across and waved their good-byes. I do not remember if I waved back. I hightailed it into the relative safety of my all-girl dorm. Lunchtime came, and I found one of the other students I had seen under the bridge.

I recounted my near miss. She looked at me and began to chuckle. "No, no," she said, "they were just making sure you got across the busy intersection safely." Excuse me? No. You mean they were not planning to abduct me?

Have you ever had the urge to disappear through the floor? I felt less than an inch tall.

I had no idea my world was about to change forever that year. I went back to my dorm room unsettled and on edge. God was messing with my comfort zones. One of the most pivotal lessons in the greatness of His love was discovering the smallness of my own. School was in session in more ways than one.

Over the next three years my greatest classroom became a street corner. I would learn about giving my life away. I would learn about the subtle power plays of being the helper instead of the helped. And I would be challenged to go as a lover and a learner choosing the lowest place of dependence and humility.

In my first few weeks at Baylor, I was planning to continue the path I had painstakingly carved out in Florida. God, however, had different ideas. I have noticed this theme. When I think I have a plan, usually God likes to turn it on its head. But His plans are always better than mine. So He sent me into a world that could not care less about my writing ability, my prestigious résumé or my so-called success. The only thing in which they were remotely interested was the answer to one question: Do you really love me?

This one single question encompasses many others: Can you look past my pain and addiction and love me anyway? Can you see beyond the masks I wear to who I really am? Will you love me even when I disappoint and hurt you?

I went from the consecrated and accessorized to the commonplace and cantankerous. And I was being drawn deeper into the Kingdom with every step.

I thought I had served my time in children's work. I had even trained other leaders. Now I got to do the real stuff with big people, right? Not even close. This time God sent me out not to teach the children, but for the children to teach me! Four days a week I gathered children from inner-city neighborhoods and housing projects for stories and songs on vacant fields and run-down playgrounds. I ventured into gang-controlled war zones that even the local police would not approach. It was here that I met some of my greatest teachers. At eight, nine and ten years old, they knew what really mattered. My prayer that became the cry of my heart began to form deep within me: *Jesus, let me love with Your love and see with Your eyes. I do not know what love looks like here.*

What did love look like to the abandoned and abused, the desperate and despised? What did love mean to the invisible and the indigent? How could I love the ones who fought the very thing they longed for the most?

One dreadfully cold winter day, we held a Christmas party for our local kids. In those days my ministry budget was about fifteen dollars a week for supplies. I operated out of the trunk of my early '90s Buick. Friends and I had gathered blankets and donated socks to give the kids for presents. We had a special treat of hot cocoa for snack time. This was a party!

My four one-time volunteers made the cocoa before we left. But they failed to let me know that they had only one standard-size orange cooler, and it was only partially full.

Our team arrived to an unprecedented turnout of kids. Eighty to ninety kids gathered in our adopted field. Soon they all were bundled together with blankets, wearing their socks like mittens, their faces smiling over steaming cups of hot chocolate.

Not knowing we had a developing cocoa supply crisis on our hands, I began to pass out overflowing twelve-ounce cups left and right. *You want seconds? No problem! Random passersby— Sure! We have enough! It is cold! Be blessed—have some cocoa!*

My volunteers' eyes grew bigger and bigger and bigger. Only later did they tell me why.

At first I thought they were kidding. I really did not believe them. They took the lid off the container to prove their point. I was speechless. What? How? Was I seeing the cocoa line just below the half-full spot? I knew how much cocoa I had passed out. I did not know what to say. It was not exactly the feeding of the five thousand. But we had the feeding of the 95.

Our mealtime miracle began to teach me that love was tangible. The Kingdom was touchable. In the middle of winter, love looked like hot cocoa freely given to those who were cold.

My love was too small. But His love was limitless. In the supernatural realm of God's Kingdom, there was more than enough. He even knew how to make hot cocoa in Texas.

My Presence Is Your Home

A few years later God told me to move to Calcutta, India. I did not have a mission agency. I knew one person there, who, it turned out, had to leave the country three weeks after I arrived. I had spent a semester abroad in the villages of Bangladesh in 1997 serving in a children's home, so I thought I knew what I was getting into. The beauty of the villages in rural Bangladesh was far removed from the blatant poverty in the urban sprawl of Calcutta, then teeming with eighteen million people. Calcutta is named after the Hindu deity Kali, goddess of death and destruction. You become like that which you worship. Need I say more?

The flat where I lived alone was almost directly above a small slum. The minute I walked outside my gate I was greeted by children begging. Some had eyes plucked out or limbs cut off to make them more profitable for the mafia rings that controlled them.

My daily course took me through a maze of streets and alleys to find simple things like bread and milk. I walked through human excrement on the streets. I stepped over the dying. I stopped and looked into the eyes of the demonized clawing at my clothes. Street children thronged me for money or food. I practiced my Bengali sitting in the mud with the women as they washed clothes. I enjoyed curry and chai, mangoes and masala. I reveled in the smiles and laughter of the street children who became my friends.

I shared Jesus with beggars on the corners who wondered why I was not in my country begging. I had one leg; I should be in my country begging, and I definitely should not be happy. I introduced them to the One who took care of my needs and gave me joy. There in Calcutta I learned that some of my favorite places were slums and leper colonies.

One night, the sounds of the death drums shook the walls of my little flat. It was *puja* season. As the worshipers chanted outside my door and beat rhythms honoring destruction, I packed and tried not to be ill. I was getting ready to go teach at some meetings in Bangladesh. I put on a teaching tape about encountering God and turned it up loudly to drown out the ruckus below. As I sorted and folded clothes, the presence of Jesus entered my small room and became stronger and stronger until I could no longer pack.

I fell to my face and began to weep. I was sick. I was discouraged. I was overwhelmed. I had never seen such pain and suffering. It hurt to have eyes to see. All my plans and expectations had been shredded in front of me. I was on my own. My primary sending church had just crumbled due to leadership problems. I had rats in my flat. I was dirty most of the time. The loneliness in my heart went far deeper than location.

Then I heard Jesus whisper one simple little line that changed my life: *My presence is your home. Your home is in My heart.*

That night I began to discover the depths of my own need. In that foreign landscape where dirt, death and poverty embrace beauty, hope and compassion in a wild dance of contradiction and paradox, I saw my first glimpse of home. I did not find it in Calcutta, nor did I find it in Colorado, where I moved after I left India. I was beginning to learn that my home was not about geography at all.

The Beauty of a Wasted Life

She was like many of the street girls I met in Calcutta. In fact, that is what drew me to her story. She spent her life earning a living by selling false love to any who would buy it.

But the Man before her now was different. He looked past her reputation to her very soul. His eyes held no agenda, no desire to use her. They probed the deepest crevasses of her pain, but she saw no loathing, no hatred, no condemnation. How could this be? She saw only compassion and mercy mingled with sadness at what He knew she had suffered.

She looked away. She did not know what to do in the face of a love that held no guile or hidden motive. Yet her gaze drew back to this Man they called Teacher. Her heart compelled her. Could it really be true? One more time their gazes locked. She could not look away again, even if she tried. How could she return even a drop of the ocean of love in which He washed her that day? It was inappropriate, to be sure. It was in the middle of an important dinner for which she had no invitation. And it was not in the proper manner. She could scarcely believe she had just barged right into the middle of the room. It was absolutely undignified. Yet she was compelled by His love. She washed His feet with her tears and wiped them with her hair.

It cost her everything: every shred of dignity and a year's wages gone in an instant as she poured out her precious perfume. Did they know how this aroma had been earned? She shuddered at the thought. But it was fleeting. The look in His eyes again captured her heart. The room disappeared. The jeering looks and accusations faded as He filled all her vision.

Wasteful, indignant extravagance poured over this Man, the only Man who ever showed her the face of love. How could she not pour out her everything on Him?

Love outpoured overtook the gathering. The fragrance of intoxicating, overpowering adoration that gave all it had and risked all it was filled the room. Inappropriate. Indecent. Scandalous. Wasteful.

But Jesus—what did He do? He accepted it. He defended it. He applauded it. He cherished it. He recorded it for all time.

Can one glance, I thought, *one encounter with Him so change your life? Can one meeting with this Man Jesus be so dangerous that you would gladly lose your reputation for one more moment in His presence? Is it possible to be so in love that your life wasted in worship makes history?*

I did not know. But I decided something in the back alleyways of Calcutta amidst the broken and the dying. I decided something as the lepers' weeping sores oozed onto me, as I held the ones called untouchable. It did not come all at once, but slowly a resolution formed in my heart.

Somehow my goals had changed. Success looked different reflected in the eyes of the poor and the broken. My desire became to learn to live in His heart of love. My goal became to waste my life. I had no other pursuit. Not anymore. Not since Jesus captivated my gaze.

Benia's Cry

I left India in 2002. Four years later I arrived to meet my then 35 children and a few miscellaneous adults in Sudan. How I got there in the fall of 2006 is quite the story; we will get to it soon enough in the next chapter. But right now, I want you to meet Benia (not her real name).

We were eager to kick off our first real worship service together in our newly formed little fellowship. As I scanned the small gathering, I saw them all the way in the back of the dimly lit room: four little girls with their heads hung low staring at some invisible item of fascination on our dirt floor; two women, their stares fixed into the vacant space of grief; and one slight man with a lifetime of pain etched into his not yet forty-year-old face. I went back and welcomed our visitors, as was our custom.

We continued with worship, and I shared some simple message about God's love. Our kids poked each other and giggled through our time together, and we dismissed. Our service contained no flash or elegance; it was just family loving Him and learning what it means to love one another.

Once again I made my way to the little group in the back of the room and introduced myself. After 45 seconds I had exhausted all the Juba Arabic I knew and called one of our older kids over to help translate. Through muted words and long silences filled with shame, they shared their story.

The four little girls had lost their mother. Mama had been very, very sad. One day she took some rope and threw it over the support beam in their tukal. She hanged herself to escape the pain in her heart. Her heart never found its home. Now her four small girls—ages six, four, two and four months—were asking if they could come live in ours.

My eyes teared up as I heard their tragedy and saw the heavy weight of shame on their shoulders. A friend who was visiting at the time was bouncing the youngest: Benia. Little did we know that she was going to teach us about the reality of true worship.

Our family grew by four more that day. And I began a new lesson on what it means to become the face of love. After a few days, the family helper had the girls settled and went home. This meant I inherited the care of Benia, then four months old.

Now let me give you a little context. I am an only child. Prior to coming to Africa the longest contact I had had with an infant was to hold one in a prayer line or babysit for a friend for a few hours. We had little Ima with us, but one of our Sudanese mamas looked after him. I had no idea what God had just gotten me into. And Benia was no ordinary baby.

No doubt Benia was traumatized by her mother's death. But her wounds went far deeper. I looked into her little eyes and saw eyes that did not belong to her looking back at me. It was disconcerting, to say the least. It definitely messed with my theology.

Southern Sudan, while popularly believed to be Christian, is really more animistic than anything. Some of our Sudanese leaders estimate as little as 3 percent of people here truly know Jesus, regardless of what they call themselves. Witchcraft and traditional folk ritual have so interwoven themselves into the fabric of life here that even the Christianity present is often mixed.

Benia cried for three weeks straight. For three weeks I had no sleep. For three weeks I watched her look at me calculatingly with a gaze not her own and then swipe her small nails at my face, aiming for my eyes. My friend who was visiting and helping us at that time was the eldest of five children and assured me that this was not normal baby behavior. We had a possessed infant on our hands.

What was the appropriate response in the face of such anger and hate coming from a four-month-old? A screaming, authority-declaring exorcism session? I think not. This was a hurting baby. Was this evil presence tormenting our newest little one going to be shouted out of her? No. It was going to be loved out.

Hate cannot stand in the face of love. The answer was to love her past the place of her pain and oppression, to become the face of His love. So we held her and rocked her and dodged her swipes. We blessed her and loved her and sang over her.

One week, two weeks, three weeks. Love takes time. It is not to be hurried. Love stops. Love is patient. Love suffers long and perseveres.

We entered into the high worship of laying down our sleep, laying down our meager time alone, laying down our desires and even some of our needs for the sake of another. We died. Oh, did we die. But as we died, little by little she began to live.

How did freedom come? Gradually, in an instant—I do not know. But one day she was different. One day she was so filled with love that the evil had no more room. Love cost us, but it was worth more than we could ever give. Every time I look into her chubby little grin, my heart melts. The day eight months later when she took her first steps into my arms, my spirit leapt. A princess born for such a time as this. Yes, she was worth it. Every second.

What was Benia's cry?

It was for supernatural love that was stronger than fear and pain and hate. It was for arms to hold her that would not let go, no matter what. It was for this amazing mystery of belonging where we know we are loved and cherished and safe. It was to know she had truly come home.

What is Benia's cry? It is ours.

The Face of Love

This may be a cardinal sin for a missionary to admit, but I am going to admit it anyway: I have lost my missions theology. Somehow in the middle of machine gun fire, dirt, dying children and eating beans and *posho* every day, it escaped me. It got deconstructed. I left it behind somewhere out there between nowhere and the point of no return.

But I traded it in for a theology of love. Or at least a theology of learning how to love.

What does love look like? Good news that is really good is concerned with the whole person. What does it mean to be the face of love? To the thirsty, it looks like clean water. To the hungry, it looks like food to eat. To widows, it looks like a sustainable income. To the sick, it looks like healing. To a discarded child, it looks like a home.

This love does not start with a good program. It cannot. It starts with being *in* love, being intimately connected to Jesus. It starts with knowing first that I am loved. I cannot give what I do not have. It is supernatural. It cannot be apart from Him. All living fruit in my life has come only from a living relationship with Him.

One day not too long ago I looked up at the forming clouds that signaled the end to the dry season. The rains were beginning to come right on cue. Everything in me hoped and prayed that those clouds were signifying more than just the seasons changing in the natural. In many ways it felt like a time of new beginnings. My heart longed to see a supernaturally practical display of God's love meet the many problems here with all the power and reality of heaven to bring lasting transformation.

Even in the midst of so many challenges, I take great joy in love's quiet victories, in change coming in small ways. I am delighted that Ania (not her real name), one of my little girls, who used to scream and not allow anyone to touch her, has become almost my constant companion out and about on the compound. She loves to fall asleep at night in my lap during worship. Love can be so simple. She reminds me of that. Every day I have opportunities to learn more of the power and mystery of what it means to love.

One sultry afternoon I was called to pray for a friend's daughter who was dying in the hospital. I had just entered the hospital grounds when someone shouting my name interrupted my trajectory to the ward. Some of our Congolese friends came up to me and asked me to come with them. They had a great sense of urgency and grief written on their faces. Love, even on a mission, is willing to be interrupted.

I came to discover that one of their young church members had been beaten to death by the man she had just married. I walked into the morgue with them, and her body lay cold on the cement table. The smell of death hung in the air. I placed my hand on her head and prayed and prayed for her to come back to life. She did not. So we offered the use of our truck to take her body to the burial place only two miles away, and I held some family members as they grieved. That is what love looked like in the moment.

I then went on to my original destination of the hospital ward to pray for our friend's daughter. This young woman's story had pierced my heart with compassion. She had scraped her leg on a nail and the infection that ensued took ten months but eventually ravished her body. She lay dying in a coma. The stench of rotting flesh and the accompanying flies were so severe that I felt nauseous. I went and picked up her head and spoke life into her. I prayed for her. I looked deeply into her blank stare. I quoted Scripture. I held her and sang. God was God, and I was

Michele. I had had the chance to lead her to Jesus several months before. I stood in faith with everything in me for her complete restoration. Love is not deterred by natural circumstances. It looks beyond them to God's promise and provision.

I returned home after praying. About four the next morning, I woke up to a vision of her standing with Jesus, and I knew she had gone home to be with Him. And she was very happy there. The sorrow was ours, but for her, suffering had given way to joy!

I was discovering that loving like Jesus meant a willingness to embrace His cup of suffering as well as joy. What was this cup of suffering? Was it sickness and pain and death? I do not believe so. Jesus healed the sick, bound up the brokenhearted and interrupted every funeral He ever attended, including His own! He taught us to pray "on earth as it is in heaven" for a reason. No, I believe this cup of suffering was paying the price to have eyes to see when it is easier to turn away.

The next day I was invited to preach at my Sudanese sister's funeral. About two hundred of her friends and family attended—and me, the little white woman. I still had not given up hope. Not until the last nail was in her casket. I went and laid hands on her body and prayed again. Love perseveres.

Funerals where I live can be very overwhelming affairs. Death wails often continue long into the night, and there is a sense of mourning with no hope, only despair. My heart broke to see her close relatives in dirt and ashes (literally), half clothed and wailing as though they were mad. I was proud of our mamas who care for our children. They came with me to support the family and show love to them. They understood that our sadness is not without hope. Love truly is stronger than death. In the place of great despair these precious women started to worship and sing, and soon the whole crowd was worshiping instead of wailing.

On our ride home we were bouncing down the road in our ancient white Land Rover, affectionately dubbed "Lemonade," which was held together with duct tape and ran on prayer. (When life serves you lemons . . .) I was triumphantly communicating in near sentences in Arabic as we talked about the experiences of the day.

One of our leaders told us that if he were going to start a church, he would call it *Muhabik*, or "Love." It would be all about loving Jesus and loving people just as we had been privileged to do in this situation. I loved his comment because the Church is not about where it meets or what it looks like. It is just about doing what we see Jesus doing. After all, that was all we did for our friend's family.

In the midst of a rather heavy day I drank deeply of the cup of joy. Like the coming rains, change was on its way. Our leaders were beginning to see more every day through the eyes of His love. I looked at the gathering clouds on the horizon and smiled. Change blows in fits and squalls at first. It comes imperceptibly, hanging in the air until it breaks loose around you. And it is worth waiting for.

Still the prayer I had prayed nearly every day for over a decade remained: *Jesus, let me love with Your love and see with Your eyes. Show me what it means to be the expression of Your heart to those around me.* Because I knew more than ever that His love did indeed have a face: mine.

On the road to Sudan, in Mozambique with Dr. Heidi Baker, founding director of Iris Ministries, Inc.

3 *The Unpaved Road*

The hum of our generator adds a constant harmonic drone to my thoughts. I am just grateful for the power it is feeding my laptop battery as I write. The generator is unpredictable at best, and we never know when it will work.

I think you are reading my fifteenth revision of this portion of the story. I want to tell you how I got here, but I really do not want to bore you with too many details. All journeys that really matter start deep inside of us. My journey to Sudan has been no exception. The unpaved road into Sudan that started at the last major border town in Uganda was greatly eclipsed by the unpaved road my heart had to embrace before I ever got here.

You Crazy White Woman!!!

Everyone always asks me how we have achieved such "success" in what we do: How did you grow from nothing to more than eighty children and twenty full-time staff, a school, training seminars, multiple outreaches and church plants in less than two years? What were your action steps? You had to have a plan! They all think we had a magic formula for success.

Yet I do not have a plan to give them. Honest. This story did not start with a plan. It started with a promise: "The days of dignity for you are over, but the days of demonstration are just beginning." When I received this promise, I began to learn that God desires only one thing regarding my dignity: death.

No one can see God's face and live—at least not as the same person he or she was before the encounter. And in order to see His face, to experience that kind of intimacy with Him, one must die to one's self. The day I received that promise, I began to let go of my dignity, and my life forever veered away from all paths paved. There is no paved road that leads to destiny. I began to learn that it is not about a road but about a relationship. It is not about location but about learning what it means to live in love.

Every place I went in South Africa and Uganda in 2006 on my way to Sudan, the same sentiment was repeated: "You crazy white woman! What do you think you are doing?" I remember sitting in an office in Kampala, Uganda, talking to a development agency about the situation that awaited me. Uganda borders Sudan just to its south.

"You have no plan, no strategy, no money, no contacts, no team, no anything! What—are you just going to show up? In the war-torn bush? You are out of your mind."

Well, I never claimed sanity. I am perfectly okay with being out of my mind, as long as I am firmly planted in His. I just smiled in response, sensing that such an explanation would be wasted in this case.

The slight Ugandan man wrinkled his nose and pointed his finger at me. "You could get yourself killed." I did not doubt he was right. But at the moment I was concerned more with the motorbike ride home to my guesthouse through Kampala's traffic snarl than a place I had not yet figured out how to get to.

Over the next three weeks one contact led to another, and soon I was in the northwest corner of Uganda entering Sudan's nearest border town, Arua. Before I knew it I was trundling down a washed-out, barely there road in territory plagued with problems from the LRA (the Lord's Resistance Army, a rebel group led by northern Ugandan Joseph Kony that is known for its brutality). The only foreigner and the only female traveling with a group of five people I did not know, I was moving to Yei, Central Equatoria, sight unseen.

Everyone and their cousin seemed to think I was insane. I had no feasibility study. I had a place to stay only for the first few days and the names of a few people who did not know I was coming. I barely had enough money to support myself for more than a few weeks. I had heard story upon story of Westerners who could not handle the harsh conditions. Some folded and returned home in less than a year, some with deep mental issues. I was indeed just showing up. But so was Jesus.

Yei is a dusty outback town nestled between the borders of DR Congo and Uganda. It is a commerce hub and carries with it all the vices of a trucking town. The unpaved road between Arua and Yei is frequented by bands of soldiers and thieves. After dark it can be deadly. I had heard stories of female foreigners who would not even venture off their compounds unaccompanied. In addition, the road often is impassable during rainy season, and we were driving at the height of the rains.

One point during my initial road trip was particularly harrowing. A half-mile line of trucks were stuck in the thick mud, some even overturned. The road had completely been washed out. Crowds of stranded motorists lined the roadside in squatter settlements. Tensions were so intense that the atmosphere seemed combustible.

Our driver decided to try to make the crossing with our rented Land Cruiser through the mud bog on two inverted half culverts that formed a makeshift bridge. At one point, half our car hung in midair as an army of Sudanese men sat on one side to counterbalance it until it could find traction. I sat on the side hanging over thin air and braced myself in case the car flipped. I do not know how exactly, but we made it across.

We barely had time to breathe a sigh of relief when a mob swarmed the car and began shaking it, wanting payment of twenty U.S. dollars apiece for their services. I did not have money to give them.

I looked at the man closest to me who was irate, yelling in my face in some foreign language. *Jesus, what do I do?* "I am so sorry," I told him. "I cannot give you what you ask, but you can have all the bananas we have." He snatched the bundle out of my hand, grumbled something unintelligible and left, obviously disgruntled. We drove through the hostile crowd and continued on our way.

Along the road children would run alongside our car shouting, "*Kwaja, jibu guruush.*" ("White person, give me money.")

It seemed to be the prevailing sentiment. Nevertheless I was entering into the land of God's promises, and I knew it.

The drive took almost ten hours. It offered much time for me to remember and reflect. How exactly *did* I wind up on this road? It all started almost six years earlier. On my way to India in 2000, I unknowingly stepped off the defined path to discover that the inner pursuit of God's heart was just as unpaved as the roads in Sudan—if not more so.

God, Give Me Everything They Have!

I grew up in the Episcopal church. I was christened twice, was confirmed once and started to sing in the choir at nine. In high school I defected to the Baptist church across the street because they said they knew "how to do" missions.

I went to a renewal service once by accident when I was nineteen. I thought the people all looked like a bunch of Mexican jumping beans and wondered if we needed to call 9-1-1 for the people falling down at the front. I subsequently visited the Brownsville Revival in its heyday several times and was moved. I felt God's presence, but didn't everyone?

I tried to figure out where I fit on the label spectrum. A Pentecostal–Baptist–evangelical–liturgical–renewed–international lover of Jesus—would that work? After a season of trying to figure out what I was, I decided to give up on labels. I mean, Jesus did not seem to need one. I never read that Jesus even called His followers *Christians*. The world gave them that label. Maybe Jesus never came to make Christians, I surmised. Maybe He just came to show us the way to our Papa, Father God in heaven. I figured it was good enough to be in love. So if people asked me what I was, that became my general reply: I am in love.

My journey deeper into God's heart took a dramatic turn in 2000 as I was about to leave for Calcutta, India, to give my life away among the poor. Someone handed me a magazine article about an outpouring in the city of Toronto and the subsequent revival in Mozambique. I had never heard of the "Toronto Blessing," as it was called.

I looked at the magazine that had been handed to me, admittedly with a bit of disdain. I shook my head at all the glossy ads. *How many hungry people could eat off the money spent on this one ad?* I thought. I used to be uptight about things like that, in theory at least. If the poor could not eat cheese or have a Coke, then neither would I. If they ate day-old rice, then I would suffer with them. God has loosened me up since then. Miserable missionaries are not very effective.

As I dutifully gave the magazine a cursory once-over, my eyes landed on an article about this little blonde woman wearing a skirt who was baptizing an African child in a feed trough filled with murky greenish water. I skimmed the photos of the children in worship. The supernatural was happening all around this woman somewhere in Africa. I began to read the first few paragraphs.

Mama Aida, as she was called, had received a seven-day visitation from Jesus in this Toronto Airport service. As I stopped to try to figure out how they got past security to meet in an airport (they do not actually meet in an airport), I began to feel this warmth like liquid fire swirling in my stomach. Then the room began to spin. My hands began to shake, and I felt like Jell-O.

God, I am leaving for India—I cannot be getting sick. But I was not sick. I did not at first realize that what I was encountering was an all-out invasion of His Spirit. As it began to dawn on me, out of the depths of my spirit I cried, *God, give me everything they have!* I had no idea what I was asking. But He did!

I forced myself off the floor where I was sitting and put the magazine in a box in the closet, never reading the rest of the article. I continued getting ready to leave, all the while fighting back tears and trying to shake off this strange stirring in my spirit. As my plane departed I prayed, *God, You are no respecter of airports. You could meet me in Heathrow! You did not tell me to go to Toronto or Africa; You told me to go to India. You are God, and I want everything of You those places have!*

My time in India taught me many things. It taught me that some of my favorite places are slums and leper colonies. It taught me about the greatness of God's mercy and compassion. And it taught me about the smallness of my own.

Where Only Dead People Will Go

While I lived in Calcutta serving the poor, deep inside something in me thought, *Ahhh, it would be nice to have a successful ministry with a glossy brochure one day. It would be wonderful to have a car and a lovely house and to do something not so, well, stretching.*

Well, God in His great mercy sent me to the land of successful ministries with glossy promotional materials. From India He directed me to spend the next few years in Colorado Springs, a land of nice cars and lovely homes that is a ministry

Mecca for evangelical Christendom. He gave me a taste of the things I thought I wanted, and I quickly learned that what I thought I wanted did not make me happy. They did not satisfy the desires of my heart. They did not give me life. Colorado Springs was everything I was not but was secretly trying to become—until I lived there. In this beautiful ministry Mecca, my heart shriveled up.

In Colorado Springs the only ministry I could "do" was graphic design, which felt relatively useless. Still trying to be dignified, I concocted plan after plan to "be successful." Yet every plan I designed blew up in my face. God relentlessly put a stop to every effort I made, and I achieved nothing but growing frustration. I began to try to sneak out of the season God had me in there. Central Asia? Sign me up! The Middle East? When do I leave? I was wasting away as I began to discover I was created for wastelands and war zones in the middle of a place that was the farthest thing from them. Colorado Springs did not even have a decent inner city. I would drive to Denver just to find an urban reality and would purposefully hang out in nearby Manitou Springs, then an occult headquarters for the United States, just to find someplace with an edge.

One year, two years, three years: *God, this is killing me to be here!*

Good, because where I am about to send you only dead people will go.

I was learning God's qualification process for greatness, and ultimately Colorado was a great place to die to self. I, as I had lived before, stopped being. I began to realize that only when I live inside Him can He fully live inside me.

Let's face it. Dead people are really hard to embarrass and impossible to scare. They have to live from another realm because they no longer exist in the present one. They do not have any opinions, and they are absolutely unoffendable. They listen more than they speak. You can step on their toes and it does not bother them one bit. They see beyond the seen into the eternal unseen. And they have no concern for their reputation. Personal dignity means nothing to them. They make great cross-cultural ambassadors.

God was indeed killing me. He was provoking me to desperation. All my plans were being dismantled piece by piece to make way for His promise. Holy desperation became the context for holy demonstration. Dignified has never changed the world. Desperate has.

Always Enough

What an infuriating title for a meeting, I thought. "There Will Always Be Enough." Where did they get that one?

These thoughts ran through my head like marathon racers as I debated whether or not I should attend the House2House Conference in Denver in 2005. I looked at my latest bank statement and fumed. I felt as though there was never enough! I could not even afford the conference fees.

But somehow it worked out, and I arrived at the conference to find that the keynote speaker was a man named Rolland Baker from Iris Ministries. The magazine article I had read five years earlier flashed across my mind: These were the people I had read about on my way to India! *God, what are You setting up here?* I had no clue that my days in Colorado were rapidly coming to a close.

As Rolland spoke of God's heart and the simplicity of the Gospel, I saw a reality, an authority and a joy I had never seen in anyone. I was hungry. I was not at all patient. For the first time I heard someone describe my heart of hearts, and I was undone. I could not wait to respond. My heart felt as if it was exploding. I did not know what to do.

So before he had fully finished his message, I dive-bombed the altar. I left my crutches at my front-row seat, took a great flying leap and slid into place on my face on the floor—rug burn, tears and all.

Long after the meeting was over friends helped me into a waiting area in the ladies' room. We were in an elegant hotel—the kind that has carpeted sitting rooms with couches in the "powder" area. I was a shaking mess who could not walk in a straight line, and they thought it was best I wait it out in a less visible place. I was horrified. Undone in public. Sweet Jesus, have mercy. Yet the power of God was still so powerful and tangible that the entire room was filled with it.

The little Chinese maid came in to clean and asked if we needed assistance. Logical conclusion. As time passed she kept coming back to check on us. One of my friends *happened* to speak Cantonese, and we were able to lead her to Jesus. She brought her friends back a little while later for prayer, and we had a mini-outpouring in the ladies' room. I think I finally made it up to my room about 3:00 A.M.

Over the next seven days, God undid me. He took me apart and put me back together. He rewired my thinking. He breathed life into my DNA. He forever smudged my polish and demolished my plans. He called forth the core of who I was. I was about to find out: There was not just always enough; there was always more. And it truly was all about love.

Uh, God? Sudan Is in Africa

My undoing had only just begun. I entered into a whirlwind of change and transition, and it only intensified from there. Within seven weeks of that fateful encounter in Denver, I was preparing to move back overseas. In the ensuing months I handed over my leadership position in a growing international ministry, resigned from my MBA studies at the local university, gave notice on my lease and began to research flights from Denver to Calcutta.

Yes, India. My focus was still set on Asia. Sudan was a story I saw on a PBS special and shed tears over. But it did not have any practical place in my scope of vision. Africa was simply the continent I flew past on my way to get to India.

Ah! That flight will work! I thought as I gazed at flight information on my computer screen. I got out my credit card, ready to make the purchase, and once again my plan got adjusted.

Beloved, I am glad you love India. I love India. I have great plans for India. But will you let Me send you to Sudan instead?

The room began to spin, not unlike five years earlier in Florida.

Jesus, (gulp) *Sudan is in Africa.*

Yes, I know. (I am glad God knows His geography.)

But, Jesus, that is another continent.

I looked into His eyes and saw reflections of the number one worst place on the planet, according to many statistics. Over five decades of almost continual civil war, where millions of lives have been lost and millions more displaced, where a whole generation does not know what peace looks like, a place where the infrastructure has been decimated, where rape and mutilation have been used as weapons of war, where race and religion have combined in a power struggle that has devastated the largest geographical country on the continent of Africa— would I go there?

I had seen His eyes. How could I not?

I never would have guessed that I would trade my comfortable apartment in Colorado for the unknown path that led me deeper into the heart of Africa with every step. My relationship with Rolland (and subsequently his wife, Heidi) that started by my interrupting his message at that pivotal conference had led me to their doorstep.

Undone by Love

My journey to Africa was not without its fair share of challenges. The weekend before I left Colorado, an eighteen-wheeler came over on top of my 1997 Buick LeSabre, forcing me off the road. I walked away shaken up but without a scratch. I could not say the same for my car. Then on my flight from the United States to London, I came down with shingles, a painful nerve-ending virus related to chicken pox. I went to see a physician's assistant in Tanzania on my way to Mozambique, only to have him tell me that I might have a suppressed immune system and should consider returning to the United States immediately.

I arrived in Pemba, the home of the Holy Given School of Missions at Iris Ministries, tired, in pain and sick. But I was determined. No virus or immunodeficiency threat was going to keep me from His promise. I would not be deterred. I believed for complete healing. And God came through.

I do not remember much of the teaching. (Sorry, Heidi, Rolland, Lesley-Anne and family.) What I remember is three months of living in the light of His face. I was being submerged into the reality of His love in which I was being called to live. For those who think visitations from God are all warm, fuzzy and convenient, let me assure you they are not. Sometimes it is more as though He comes and sits on you to make a point. Several times I felt God's presence so strongly that I was stuck to the grass mat/dirt floor and unable to move. His liquid, weighty, heavy glory love was like a thick blanket, and I could not even lift my hand off the ground.

One afternoon while experiencing this kind of power of the Holy Spirit, friends kindly moved me out of the sun into the shade under the green-and-white-striped tent where we met for our classes. I was not able to move for over five hours. At one point I realized children were dancing in worship around me and kicking me in the head. Lovely. I still could not move.

I am a do-er. I like to be busy. I like to accomplish things. My life could have capitalized the "A" in Type A personality. But that summer in Pemba, Jesus was showing me there was nothing that I could do to produce His promise in my life.

As I lay there unable to move with children joyfully kicking my head, He spoke: *Beloved, this is exactly what you are going to be able to do in Sudan*—[pause]—*nothing. But as you lay down, I will stand up in you and do more in a day than you can dream of doing in a decade.*

If I had any shred of dignity left, my time in northern Mozambique definitely removed that, too. I spent the summer face-planted in the dirt, being electrocuted by His intensity, often weeping and sometimes laughing as His love saturated every cell of my being. All I wanted was Jesus. I could not get enough of Him. The preparation of desperation had been unleashed into my life in full force.

I was completely undone by love. I was learning the rhythm of His heartbeat. All my studies of systematic scriptural interpretation, Greek and Hebrew exposition and practical cross-cultural missiology were reduced to loving God and loving the person in front of me.

That was what my summer in the dirt was all about: an interior quest for the depths of His heart to be realized in mine. Yet again my original visions of what I thought my call in Sudan would look like were carefully undone, right along with me. By the time I left Pemba in August 2006, all I had was a promise to hold on to!

Applause for Abram

Where exactly I was going was anyone's guess. I started to sympathize with Abram. Imagine waking up one day to God telling you to get up, leave everything and go to a land you have never seen, where you know no one and you do not even have a set destination. *Just trust Me, Abram. Go to the land I will show you.* I applauded Abram's trust in God, but following in his steps was an entirely different matter altogether. As I left Mozambique for the unknown, I got the rare opportunity to explore Abram's spiritual footprints.

My next stop took me down to South Africa. God said to go to Johannesburg and pray for three weeks. That did not make much sense to me, but again God is God, and I am not. I have discovered He does indeed know what He is doing. I wound up in a little upper room in a dilapidated building in the inner city of Johannesburg.

I had been told Johannesburg is known for having the highest murder rate in the world. It was a place feared by most, and there I was staying in its equivalent of Harlem—alone. The building was so old that it almost burned down around me due to electrical problems. I spent my days walking the neighborhood, talking to people. I was enjoying getting to know the precious Muslim Punjabi family down the street who made the most delicious *biriyani* I had had since leaving India. I talked to the kids on the corners and the young girls in the nearby beauty shop. I prayed for three weeks, and not much seemed to happen.

Then one night it all changed. Eternity invaded in an instant. One moment I was plugging away on sheer faith and raw obedience, and the next moment God manifested Himself in a fashion only He could think up.

Jesus came and stood before me. Flashes of lightning coming from inside Him filled the room. They bounced off the paneled walls and hid the peeling paint. It was one of the most extreme encounters I have ever had. My response was a reflex: I fell to my face on the stained carpet, oblivious of the mice scuttling around the periphery of the room. It was so bright I could see the flashes through my closed eyelids. As I was wondering if I would survive the experience, Jesus began to explain what was happening.

He told me that He carried the lightning of heaven in His being. Why? Because lightning was where heaven finds a place of agreement with the earth.

Then came the science refresher. He reminded me that in a lightning strike, the electrical charge first reaches up from the earth, and then what we see as lightning is heaven reaching down to meet it in visible response.

His life is in perfect agreement with heaven. This was true when He physically walked the earth, and it is true now as He lives in us. Whoever lives in love lives in God and God in him.

The lightning subsided, but He continued to share many things with me, including the direction to go to Yei. Time was overshadowed by eternity, and the eternal Now of who He is enveloped who I am.

I would love to live *in* the place of continuous visitation. But I was learning I had to live *from* the place of encountering His heart so I could carry His heart with me.

Three Little Steps

As I mentioned earlier, people always want to know how we have achieved such success in the mission field. Recently a visitor asked me for a copy of our strategic plan. It was all I could do not to burst into outright laughter. Strategic? Hmmm . . . how about spontaneous? Planned? Not at all.

The visitor was persistent. Knowing that I was not going to get anywhere unless I gave him an answer, I had an inspiration.

"Okay, are you ready?"

"Yes."

"Here are three steps to success. Do you have a pen? You will want to write these down."

He was on the edge of his seat. Expectation hung in the atmosphere.

"Step 1: *Every morning wake up*. Write that down."

His expression looked a little uncertain, but he obediently took notes.

"Step 2: *Ask Jesus what He is doing that day—not what He wants you to do, but what He is already doing.*

Love knows no limits

"Step 3: *Go join Him.*"

There they are: the three steps to ministry success. You now have my life secret to the unpaved road. These little steps led me down a trail that was unmarked with a destination that was largely undefined.

Destiny was not a destination; it was a Person. He was my destiny. His heart was my goal. The journey deeper into His love was my success.

So how did this theory work? Pretty well, if you ask us. Us? Oh, you thought I went to Sudan alone? Forgive me if I forgot to mention that I really am on a team of four: Father, Son, the Holy Spirit and me! They all live with me as I live in them, and we do everything together. And because of that, the three steps to success worked just perfectly!

A Life Possessed

My first *hour* in Sudan I met the man who owns the building we rented for two years until it was time to move onto the land God prepared for us. Within my first week (and after a team consultation), I had signed a lease. The rent to which I agreed cost more each month than I had with me at the time. The building looked utterly ludicrous and flew in the face of every inch of common sense I had. But if I had been operating purely on common sense, I would never have moved to Africa in the first place.

I hired some contractors to make it minimally livable. After six weeks of renovations on our rented facility, we opened our doors on Christmas Day 2006. Jesus asked me what I wanted to do for my first Christmas in Sudan. My answer was to throw a huge party. I love feasts. I love parties. I love seeing hungry people eat. So does He.

How many people did I want to invite? Hmmm, I think I have faith for a thousand. So we printed one thousand invitations. With the help of my new Sudanese friends, who were ecstatic about helping me execute this plan, I showered the city with invitations.

Since supplies in Sudan cost three to four times as much as they do in Uganda (if one can even find what he or she needs), I had to go to Uganda to shop. It is a trip that jars every bone you have. I arrived not feeling too well, but I figured it was road wear. The second day I thought I had the flu. By day three, what I thought was the flu rapidly disintegrated into a nasty case of malaria. But I pushed on anyway. Half conscious, I bought out the plastic market (one thousand plates and cups, thank you).

I was talking to Rolland, who knew way more about malaria than I did, on the phone, and he was looking at flight maps in consideration of airlifting me out. Unbeknownst to him and against medical advice, I sneaked back into Sudan. I was not missing Christmas dinner! And we had planned to take in our first children upon my return. No! I was going home, and that was that.

I must keep my guardian angels working overtime. We were delayed by road conditions and reached Yei around 9:00 P.M. It can be dangerous to be out at night here. Armed men with anger issues toting AK-47s often wander about with a gun in one hand and a bottle of booze in the other.

We had cleared our papers at the border. We had no idea we were supposed to stop in Yei, too. Soon after arriving in Yei, a motorbike came screaming up beside my open window with an irate, livid, drunken man holding a loaded and cocked AK-47 to my head yelling at me that I was dead. We were dead. We had made a mistake, and now he was going to kill us.

They dragged us back to the government yard and pointed their guns at us, threatening to take all we had and shoot us. I was not sure whether to laugh, cry or throw up on their shoes. I was seriously sick at the time and was trying not to pass out. Before you kill us, could you please tell us what our mistake was? This went on for over an hour until, of course, we were told that if we paid a hundred dollars we would be let go. I talked them down to eighty.

Welcome home to Sudan. Over the next few days we bought the Christmas cow that would become our dinner. We were literally planning to kill the fatted calf. Then we lost the cow, we found the cow, our contractors stole all our money and did none of the work and I remained weak and sick. But Christmas dinner was going to happen.

We had blanketed the city with paper and radio announcements. Despite the press, only a few hundred people showed up at first. So I sent out our volunteers to call in everyone they could find until all the food was gone. We took in our first twelve children and opened our doors by feeding one thousand people. The city had never seen anything like this. We had the poorest of the poor eating with U.N. officials and community leaders. We shared about another feast, one where servant lovers of Jesus will run to the ends of the earth calling in the ones He loves.

No, my story in Sudan did not start with a plan but with a promise.

But how did the promise I saw become the reality I walked in? How did this mystery of grace unfold? I believe I walked into His promise one step at a time.

One little step at a time He led me so far inside His heart of love that all my life became lived hidden in Him. I began to see more like He sees and love like He loves. It really was simple. It was Jesus. It was seeing through His eyes. It was loving with His heart. It was doing what I saw Him doing. No more, no less. It was spending enough time face-to-face with Him that I began to look like Him to the world around me.

One step at a time I said yes. Not because I had to, but because I was overtaken by His love. I said yes and yes again until there was no "no" left. It was only Him. It was His grace, His mercy, His power, His bill, His idea. Even my yes was a gift from Him!

Day by day, I was learning to live in the place of His embrace. My heart's desire became to wake up one day and find that I not only lived out of His promise but had become fully possessed by His presence.

A good plan will never change a nation. But a life possessed by God just might.

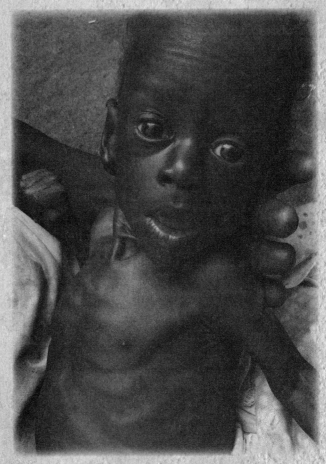
Finding treasures hidden in darkness

4 Castles in the Dirt

I once was told that it is best for a writer to write about what he or she knows. Having found this to be wise advice, I want to tell you a little more about an inescapable reality here in the outback of Sudan: dirt.

It is everywhere. It covers everything. A person in Sudan cannot sleep in his or her bed without a thin layer of dust settling on him or her. When he or she steps out of bed, it is usually onto a dirt floor. Dirt occupies whole meeting agendas from government committees to aid agencies. The topic might be called sanitation, but the bottom line is dirt and how to get rid of it. It is the subject of classes in school (hygiene) and public health seminars in the field (more hygiene).

We are largely sheltered from dirt in the westernized developed world. We have spent great amounts of time and money on annihilating its existence. Whole aisles in our supermarkets are devoted to its destruction. But here in the outback of Sudan it is an unavoidable part of life.

Cathedrals of Mud

Indeed we know a little about dirt in Africa. In fact, we even build with it. We call it *mudding*. Mudding is just what it sounds like: Mix together water and soil to make mud. Slap the blend into a pre-constructed bamboo frame until all the holes are filled. Add a roof of some variety. Make a floor of pressed dust, and if you are really going for style, smear the outside walls with cow dung to make them semi-water resistant. Ta da!—one mud house ready for occupation.

When we build with mud and straw and call it a home, it is temporary. A good wind is all it takes to destroy it and cause its occupants to rebuild. Many of those we love here cannot afford to build any other way. If a storm blows rain hard enough at the right angle, their mud *tukals* can be washed away in a day. *Kalaas*, finished. They have to start over.

When we take the time to form the dirt by hand, however, fire it into bricks and build on a foundation, our home becomes permanent. The wind and rain can pound away, but the house remains unmoved.

For twenty-plus years no one bothered with permanent structures. They were at war. Women were being raped, children abducted, villages bombed. No one worried about anything but survival in times like those. Now the war has for the moment subsided, and people are turning their attentions to rebuilding what was lost and moving ahead into the future.

One day I was *footing* through a village. That is Sudanese English for walking. For me it is an especially fitting term, as I truly am "footing." (I only have one foot, remember?) In the middle of a bustling, international metropolis of mud huts, God began to talk to me about castles in the dirt. The irony of His timing did not escape me for an instant. He told me that it is not about what I build around me. It is what He is building inside of me that matters.

I have learned here in Sudan that it is possible to build really amazing edifices with mud and a bit of know-how. The Sudanese even have cathedrals made of mud! I am not exaggerating; I have spoken in them. But no matter how grand the physical structure, they all will ultimately fall down in time.

God has shown me that the same is true in the spiritual realm. Elaborate structures of careers, organizations, programs—even ministries—are nothing more than mud houses if they are not the overflow of an inner reality of His love inside of us. I am not talking about castles made *of* dirt. I am talking about the castle of His presence that God builds *in* the dust of our lives. As we yield to Him, He is able to create in our little vessels of clay dwelling places for His glory. Ultimately that is what this book is about: a journey down an unpaved road into yielding a little more to His heart every day until our clay vessels are so transformed that we become the message we are called to bring. We become the expression of His love to the world in the places of their pain.

But Clay . . .

There have been many days that have reminded me I am but clay—many days that have proven I am nothing more than a bit of dust that God formed and into which He breathed His life. The only thing that transforms my life into a castle for His glory is, well, His glory.

Let me share a few of our daily adventures with you. It would not be fair to tell you about all the miracles and supernatural encounters without also describing to you the moments when I have wondered what in the world I am doing here at all.

God has given us forty acres of land. While the land has been an incredible blessing, some of the circumstances surrounding its acquisition have been quite challenging. One does not purchase land per se here; rather, one makes a usage agreement with the community. That is a fine concept, except when certain community members are out for every penny they can squeeze out of your bank account.

Part of our land agreement was to dig a well for the community in a certain place out in the bush. This took some time to arrange. Finding a spare ten thousand dollars did not come without some planning. Even after the financing became available, we faced the next challenge: trying to find the right drill rig and getting it to the area. Another few weeks passed as we tried to work out the logistics.

Patience is at times a poorly cultivated virtue the world over. People want what they want, and they want it right now. I did understand their predicament. Lack of clean water is a huge problem here. But the community practically had a price on my head until they got their well. Since we did not deliver immediately, certain community members assumed we were cheating them and hired witch doctors and rogue "pastors" to curse us actively. How they thought this would help their cause I do not know.

Many things mysteriously began to go wrong on our land. All our construction workers got sick at once. I came down with a bacterial infection that was serious enough to seek treatment in another country. Our indigenous director began a fight for his life with inoperable cancer. A rash of mysterious illnesses swept our children's compound.

In addition to all this, a man demanded that we compensate him for his trees that were on our land. Fair enough. Did you know that a half-dead banana tree in Yei, Sudan, goes for a whopping fifty U.S. dollars? Yessirree, you would think his trees grew gold instead of fruit. After we paid him, however, people came onto the land, burned or cut down all the trees we bought and then began to demand more money—for what we were not sure.

So-called county workers came that same week and demanded that our students pay them school fees to which they were not entitled, as we are a private church school. Also that same week we took in five displaced children from clear across the country who desperately needed homes and spoke only an unreached tribal language. Add to all this three different ministries wanting us to help finance their endeavors, an economy in turmoil and only a fraction of the money needed for our ministry coming in the past month, and you can see that I was looking out over a veritable storm-tossed ocean of need.

I did not understand it. I became increasingly frustrated as important documents went missing due to nonexistent organization, the Internet was barely accessible, I was walking in mud up to my (one) knee and my children seemed to have a penchant for demolishing everything in sight. I wanted to run away. I wanted to scream. I wanted to pull out my hair. Could this clay carry His glory?

Before I came to Sudan the Lord warned me that there would be nothing I could do here. He was right. And faced once again with a situation in which I could do absolutely nothing, I was reminded that I, Michele, could do nothing here. This has been a hard lesson for a recovering Type A personality.

Jesus has been faithful. Somehow in my weakness He has been strong. Somehow when I have thought I could not look at another bloodied toe, wipe another snotty nose, face another person begging for money, be Mama one more minute, He has come through. He awoke me in the middle of the night and told me word for word how the people were cursing us. I knew that when the well was installed there would be a meeting with the elders of this particular community, and I considered sharing some of what God showed me. But the Lord said no. He told me to bring them a message of His love. As soon as I became aware of their antics and we prayed accordingly, things improved—slowly.

It is days like these when I remember I am but clay. It is days like these when a future as that Starbucks barista looks intensely inviting. How did I wind up here after all? Oh, I remember. I said yes to the Lord. I may be a simple clay vessel, but the Father is pleased to let His glory be carried in earthen clay vessels who have said yes. And yes can be a dangerous little word. Days like these are actually quite useful, because if I did not have them, I might forget that the glory is His. I am but clay.

Remember Benia? She is almost two now. When I was at my lowest she crawled up into my lap to remind me why I am here. As she giggled, played with my fingers and looked up at me with her innocent baby grin, my interior fuming melted. I knew that I would not want to leave Sudan unless she could come, too. I want to see her grow up. It is my secret hope to be able to marry her to the man of her dreams one day in about eighteen years. Applications to Starbucks will just have to wait.

Storm Dancing

We have had our stormy seasons here, to say the least. But one cannot practice storm dancing without a storm in which to dance.

As I mentioned, one of our key leaders has been battling cancer, and I went for a month barely able to keep liquids down from some mysterious infection. During this time Uganda, DRC and southern Sudan declared war on the Lord's Resistance Army (LRA). Nothing like an international conflict practically in your backyard to make life more interesting.

The rebels were in our territory at the time, and the news on the street for several days was that they threatened to attack Yei. The atmosphere was so thick with tension you could have cut it and served it on a platter. Stress soufflé anyone?

It turned out, however, just to be rumor, and even if they had tried to attack it would have been a suicide mission. At one point they did get as close as thirteen miles. Main roads shut down outside of town, which sent local prices skyrocketing. A bag of sugar was going for almost one hundred U.S. dollars. No, that is not a typo.

The threat level outside of town was raised to level three, which means that if you are a U.N. aid worker you are to go out only with an armed escort and your bags packed. Level four means get out of Dodge. We are not subject to U.N. protocol per se, though we do prayerfully consider it in our planning. I happen to travel with armed escorts all the time, although they are not always visible.

It was a tumultuous time at best. As the winds of this storm grew in strength, I was reminded of Jesus sleeping through the storm on the Sea of Galilee and then commanding the storm to be still. He brought peace to the storm because He carried the reality of peace inside Himself. Through Him we, too, have authority to still storms. *Why not learn to dance with Him in the midst of the storm?* I thought. So this little clay vessel began to learn to dance on the waves with her King. I began to learn that when I take my eyes off Him even for a second I begin to sink and be overwhelmed by the deluge around me. But when my gaze is fixed on Him, the swelling waves only propel me higher and deeper into His heart.

In the middle of the height of the local conflict with the LRA, we loaded up our vehicle one morning to journey ten miles out of town into the bush. John and Noel, pastors of one of our newly adopted churches, served as our guides to their home area of Payawa. Two of the babies we were sponsoring there were failing alarmingly, and the village was at a loss for what to do. We also planned to have a healing outreach. In the back of the vehicle sat a ministry team that included seven of our kids who were on holiday from school. They had spent the night before "practicing" praying for the deaf and blind, laying hands on each other's eyes and sticking their fingers into one another's ears, commanding them to open in Jesus' name. They were ready for whatever Jesus brought us.

As we bounced down the washed-out road with ruts so deep I wondered several times if we would topple, we were keenly aware that rebels were in the area. Some might have called the trip foolish, but we were following what we saw Jesus doing. We were going storm dancing with Him. We were living out a love adventure.

We journeyed for about an hour while I received a running commentary from Noel regarding the area. He described unreached pockets of people along the mountain range that framed our backyard. We discussed the possibility of a trip through the bush to these unreached areas. My heart leapt with expectation—sign me up! I do not flourish staying on our compound. My heart and gifts best function among the unreached. I love the bush. I love the markets. I love being out there loving people. But that would be an adventure for another day, as God had already ordained one for this day.

Our truck arrived at Payawa and pulled off the road at the base of the mountain there. The area chief was waiting for us with arms and heart extended. Our entourage followed him on foot a half mile farther into the bush. The road was left far behind as we waded through shoulder-high grass and bush trees that eventually gave way to an occasional mud hut.

The chief was welcoming and even arranged his schedule especially to meet with us. It was the first time a *kawaja* had come to the area, let alone one to help two little dying babies.

The twin boys were indeed in desperate shape. Every beat of their tiny hearts could be seen framed by the ribs protruding from their frail chests. Huge sunken eyes with glassy stares did not bode well for their futures. They were dying. My heart plummeted somewhere into the nether reaches of my stomach. Concerns that the mamas in the village had not grasped the art of formula-making were well founded. It was worse than I thought.

How did outreach begin in Payawa? Milk-making 101.

I gathered the mamas around. They were not the twins' relatives; they were simply kind, illiterate village women who wanted to help when no one else would. The crowns waiting for them in heaven will put many to shame!

"See this cup? You pour boiled water into it and mix twelve spoons of formula into it, like so." We all counted together as I demonstrated. "*Wahid-itniin-talaata . . .*"

Then I had them do it. The chief even attended Milk-making 101 and was impressed that the white woman would sit in the dirt with the babies and the mamas.

After we made the formula I fed one of the twins his first properly proportioned bottle. I had to explain to them that his little tummy had shrunk because he had not had enough in it and that if he ate too much he would throw it back up. I showed them how to feed him a little, then rest, then a little more ten minutes later, and so on until his tummy opened up again.

That day in the middle of the storm, holding two dying infants with rebels only a few miles away, I was reminded that love is practical. It is not just preaching at a huge meeting and seeing God's glory fall (which I love!). It is teaching simple village ladies how to make milk so two little babies live another week. We left them with enough milk for three weeks.

After the milk lesson we moved on to our first village meeting in Payawa. Again the chief was there, along with about thirty women and children from surrounding huts. I had learned my whole introduction in Arabic, so I began with great enthusiasm. They sat patiently while I animatedly greeted them and introduced our group.

Their blank, amused and somewhat perplexed expressions let me know they were not catching the meaning. I stopped midway to discover that they spoke only Kawkwa, the local tribal language. Whoops! They were impressed anyway to see that I was learning Arabic, and they kindly applauded my progress. I knew more Arabic than they did.

With the help of a translator we continued the meeting in the local language, and I shared the story of blind Bartimaeus crying out for Jesus even when people told him to be quiet. I described how he left all he had to come to Jesus, and Jesus healed him. The chief had vision problems and wanted prayer. Our kids and I prayed for him, and his sight was restored. A woman had vision problems as well, so we asked the chief to pray for her with us, and her sight also was restored! The chief was elated. Not only was he healed, but he also was able to pray and see someone else healed.

To finish the day, the people of the village presented me with a fat, clucking chicken, a beautiful handwoven basket for sifting grain and a grass broom. I almost cried. The chicken alone is worth a month's wages for them. These mamas gave all they had and more. Every time I look at that beautiful woven grain basket in its new place of honor on one of my bedposts, I am reminded of the coming spiritual harvest.

Less than a month later I received word that the twin babies were gaining so much weight and doing so well that the village was calling it a miracle. And that it was. Miracles do tend to happen when we dance with Jesus in the middle of the storm and embrace a life of love.

"Hide in the Light"

One morning I was enjoying the emerging rays of sunshine dancing over my pillow when Jesus whispered into my thoughts: *In the middle of the night, hide in the Light. It is the safest place in the storm.*

Hide in the Light. In the midst of a potential war with Ugandan rebels when fear was tangible and unrest seemed imminent, when I wondered how I was to respond to a growing, almost suffocating darkness, Jesus gave me an answer. Those who do not know love hide in darkness. The rebel armies around us hid in the darkness and under its cover caused destruction. But we who are lovers of Jesus are to hide in the Light of who He is.

How am I to carry His light in my vessel of clay? I am to hide myself in it. No darkness can touch me as I hide in Him. He is my safe place in the storms that rage around me.

A friend of mine once told me that lighthouses are needed in only two places: in darkness and in storms. *De hagigah.* That is Juba Arabic for "It is so."

What does it mean to let Jesus build His castle in the clay of my life? How will He transform me into a reflection of His face? It might mean I will be called to stand in the darkness and dance through storms to shine His light. Storms, I have noticed, have a penchant for demolishing what I try to build through my own efforts. But if I let them they serve to strengthen what God is building on the inside of my life.

Okello taught me a lot about being light in darkness. I met him on one of those days that highlighted the clay of my vessel.

I had arrived home from an abysmally slow few hours at the Internet shack to find a tall, willowy young man sitting patiently with five children. It had been an infuriatingly frustrating day, and the last thing I wanted to do was listen to yet another plea for help. I am just being honest.

I welcomed them briefly and then went into my room to deposit my bag and breathe out the sigh of my favorite one-word prayer: *Grace.* I closed the wobbly door behind me and made my way out to my waiting guests. *There may be nothing we can do,* I resolved, *but I can at least give them the dignity of hearing their stories and praying with them.*

What I heard floored me. I was deeply humbled. This young man's light radiated from his pained appearance as he described the journey he had been on with the five children seated behind him. By the time he was finished, I practically told the kids to move into my room with me.

The five children, Didinga by tribe and language, came from four families along the Kenya border, and all had been orphaned by recent fighting in their home area in Eastern Equatoria. The young man, Okello, had been their Sunday school teacher. Their church, the only one in its largely unreached area, had disintegrated because of a corrupt pastor, and the twenty children now in their care were destitute.

He had heard of us, and God told him to come to Yei. He had by faith traveled hundreds of miles over five days, with five children not even related to him, in search of a better place for them. He had used all of his own resources.

It was all I could do to fight back tears as I heard Okello's heart for these children. He went to a government orphanage in another city on the way but said that even if there had been space he would not have left them there. The people of that orphanage did not love Jesus, he said, and he wanted these children to be loved and to grow up loving Jesus.

We literally did not have the physical space for even one more child in our facility. Yet in the face of poverty, violence, fear and the unknown, with next to nothing but his faith, this dear man gave all he had to follow Jesus clear across a war-torn nation to find a better life for these five children. I did not know what to say. I was looking at the face of God's love. What could I say but yes? We took the brother and sister to live with us, and we were able to find alternative accommodations for the remaining three boys.

Okello understood what it takes to shine light in darkness and see storms shift. He shone with the love and compassion that beats in the heart of our Father. Okello paid the price to let God build him into a castle of His presence, and he will have crowns in heaven that none of us can fathom. Okello became my teacher, and I saw a glimpse of what God has promised me. In this precious young man I saw a glimpse of the movement of storm dancers and light carriers who say yes and let Jesus build His home in them. It is believers like Okello who will see a nation changed literally from the inside out.

A Place for His Presence

There is a great deal of talk in the Church today about the visitation of God's presence. I love visitation. I pursue every encounter of God's presence that He desires to give me. But I am rapidly coming to realize that Jesus does not really want a place simply to *visit*. He does not want to be called as the plumber in an emergency. He is not looking for a one-night stand. He does not want to come and go and come and go on cue like a performer in a production. No, He wants a place where He can come and make His home. He and His Father and the Holy Spirit want to move in and be family with me. They desire to create in my life a castle fit for Themselves that They can inhabit and where They are fully welcome.

In the West we have a society that applauds and rewards performance. We celebrate mud cathedrals. Many have given their lives to building them, but they never let God build the one habitation in their lives that really matters: the one on the inside. Why have we often failed to see God's Kingdom come in power? Perhaps it is because we have not let the King prepare a place where He feels welcome to live in our lives.

I have watched mud huts disintegrate before my eyes for the last two years. It always starts with a little chip. Then the little chip becomes a hole. Soon half the wall falls down. I have seen enough of that to know that I do not want to give my life to building mud huts in any form. God is not after a cottage or a mud hut. He is after a castle built in my life as I yield to His life in me.

Sometimes transformation calls for demolition. It is not always comfortable; I do not even get to hold the blueprints. And it does not happen overnight. In his classic *Mere Christianity* C. S. Lewis describes this building process:

> Imagine yourself as a living house. God comes in to rebuild that house . . . He starts knocking the house about in a way that hurts abominably and does not seem to make sense. What on earth is He up to? The explanation is that He is building quite a different house from the one you thought of—throwing out a new wing here, putting on an extra floor there, running up towers, making courtyards. You thought you were going to be made into a decent little cottage: but He is building a palace. He intends to come and live in it Himself.[1]

Yes, King Jesus is intent upon transforming my clay vessel into a castle worthy of Himself, and it is a long, arduous process. Yet the changes God has been working in my heart are worth much more than anything they ever cost me. Even when it is dangerous, even if it costs me everything, I want to say yes to our untamable God and let Him make this little bit of clay His castle. As I say yes to Him, He begins to change the way I think and see until my thoughts, words and actions line up with heaven itself. I have discovered that when I agree with heaven, its substance transforms the circumstances around me until "on earth as it is in heaven" becomes my reality.

---

1. C. S. Lewis, *Mere Christianity* (New York: Touchstone, 1996), 176.

Castles are made for royalty. Where the King is received to live and rule, there is His Kingdom. I want Jesus to live in me. I want Him to be welcome in every area of my life. I want to be totally possessed and completely inhabited by His presence. I want to be a house where His glory dwells.

One afternoon earlier this year I came home to my children waiting patiently for me. We had been talking a lot about what it means to live Jesus' prayer "Your Kingdom come, Your will be done on earth as it is in heaven." The children had been working on a surprise for their mama.

Some of my boys eagerly led me around to the back of our school building, where I saw a miniature village they had carefully constructed from the mud. It looked like a perfect Sudanese community of mud tukals ready to be inhabited—if you were about eight inches tall. As they animatedly began to describe their mini world, I realized their miniature community represented far more than simply how to create a replica mud house:

> Mama, in our village there will be no sickness allowed, because there is no sickness in heaven. It will be a place like heaven. Everyone will learn and be happy together and love one another. Every tribe will be welcome. Jesus will be our Chief. He will come and live with us and tell us how we should live. He will take care of us and everyone will know and love Him. It will be His Kingdom village.

They understood. My ten-year-olds got it. They knew that it was not about mud huts. It was not about what they built or what they did. They could care less about their tukals. They were excited about Him. It was about preparing a place for His presence. It was about Jesus living in us and with us. Their little hands may have made mud houses, but when I looked at their hearts I saw nothing less than castles inhabited by the King of kings.

This Is Love

In the middle of a rough, stormy season where it is all too easy to miss the castle for the clay, I had the joy of meeting with some of our new pastors and friends. As we sat together talking and sharing life inside a real-life mud tukal under construction, the irony made me smile because again I was looking at His castles under construction in their lives.

As a visual introduction to our heartbeat as a family, I showed them a video about Iris Ministries. One precious older man with a gentle smile and tears in his eyes hit the proverbial nail on the head when he said:

> We have seen religion, but this is love. That is why, Mama, you are so different. No one has ever seen this here before. I am an old man. We have seen aid, we have seen religion, we have seen programs—but we have never seen love. Until now. That is why you have come.

This statement made tears stream down my face in a river of gratefulness to Jesus. It came on a day I desperately needed a reminder of why I was there, and it truly summed up my journey in many ways. Why did I stay in the midst of circumstances that on some days define the word *impossible*? This was why.

The reason things are so difficult and hard here, and even corrupt and violent at times, is that the people have never seen love before. Ever. From anywhere. They have seen hatred and war, religion and relief, but they have not encountered love. Until now.

The day that man spoke, my gaze was called up higher to the bigger picture found reflected in Love's eyes. My life shining His light. This clay becoming His castle. My call: to be the face of God's love today, tomorrow, always.

He is love. He is light. Love was created to shine, and its light was meant to be shared. Light was created for darkness. The reason it is often dark and tumultuous around me is because I am in a storm in the middle of the night, and Jesus has sent me to shine His love into the places of darkness and storms.

Why am I in a storm? Why am I in a war zone? It is where I belong. I am sent here to shine and bring the reality of another realm with me. I do not belong here because I am condemned to live in an atmosphere of darkness and turmoil. I belong here because through love I am commissioned to change it.

Village women listening to a message of hope

5 Eyes to See

As I stood in the crowd listening to a visiting speaker at an open-air meeting in the center of Yei, a small hand found its way into mine. I looked down to see a barely clad little girl, her skirt ripped almost up to the waist and her cracked local plastic sandals stitched together with thread.

I asked her name. Mary (not her real name). She huddled under my arm and stayed close the entire evening.

Truth be told, I had not wanted to go to this event. But my older children wanted to hear the visiting speaker. I knew in my spirit it would likely be more religious hype. I wanted us to be able to talk through the message together, for at the very least it would be a learning experience. So we went as a family.

At the far end of the field the visiting preacher talked about random Bible references and statistics. Amidst the numbers flying through the loudspeakers, nothing he shared showed any discernable love or concern for the people. It made me sad. The last thing Sudan needed was more religion. But he was not the reason we were there. Mary was.

A Treasure in a Field

Mary was the very picture of suffering. With no smile or laugh, almost no clothing on her ten-year-old body and shoes shredded by the rocky streets, her hand held mine in a firm grip.

I greeted her and looked into her eyes. I had an uncanny mental picture of Mary on a stage, shining with light and preaching to thousands. This child had a call and a destiny on her life. Like a moth by a flame, she refused to leave my side all night. I put my arm around her, and I could feel God's presence flowing out of me. I silently prayed for her, and I was given glimpses of what she had been through in her short life. It made my heart break.

Jesus whispered into my spirit to ask her where she stayed. Sometimes the most significant leadings of love are whispered. I asked, and she pointed behind us to the market area. Bits and pieces at a time, amidst deafeningly loud off-key music and the yelling of the speaker's message, her story was shared. Her father was dead. She had a mother, but she was staying with an auntie. She had a home—sort of—and I knew we were there for children who had no other options.

When it was time for us to go she trailed behind, trying to be inconspicuous and climb into our truck unnoticed. What kind of life did she have? On the surface, it sounded as though she had a place to stay and was in school. But she had no life in her eyes.

After we left I could not get her face or the look in her eyes as she watched us drive away out of my mind. My heart had been captured. Five minutes after arriving home, I grabbed my good friend and head mama, Eudita. She is up for sainthood for sticking with me as my faithful accomplice on such endeavors. Despite the encroaching night and the threat to our own safety, we went on foot back to the meeting grounds. As the light waned around us, the risks multiplied.

We both were silently praying the same prayer: *Jesus, bring us Mary. Let us find her.* Our focus was set and our gait determined. We walked back to where we had last seen her. Soon we were scouring the crowd of well over a thousand people, dodging in and out of the restless masses for almost ten minutes in the fading light before we spotted one lone little girl in rags.

My heart leapt! Hidden in a field we had found this little treasure for whom Jesus gave up everything.

We went up to Mary and asked her to take us to her home. I wanted to see where this precious one laid her head at night. Something was not right, and my spirit instinctively knew it.

Soon we were winding our way through the shadowy alleys and gingerly picking our steps through the piles of rubbish that settled along the uneven dirt paths.

A brisk twenty-minute walk took us through areas of town that no little girl should walk alone to the lodge where Mary stayed. The "lodge" was filled with women who, according to Mama Eudita, were likely "there for the men" in some form or fashion.

Mary slept and ate in the lodge/bar. We learned that her father had died in the war, and her mother was now alcoholic and homeless. Mary's aunt paid her school fees and gave her a roof over her head in exchange for her washing the utensils

These guys have found home

used in the bar. The aunt's children looked like cover children for magazines—perfectly dressed, fat and happy. The dichotomy could not have been more vivid. Mary was nothing more than slave labor.

That was a night of vivid contrasts. Mary came to us as the image of rejection and mourning. But in an instant all that changed. She was found. I felt the heart of Jesus bursting with joy that in a field where the platform ministry was about numbers and credits as the suffering looked on in silence, His treasure was found.

When I returned home from finding Mary, our children and I talked about the evening as I nursed blisters from a shoe in which I did not plan to walk over two miles. Their hearts were precious and their spirits discerning: "There was lots of dancing, Mama, but they did not talk about knowing Jesus like you do. We want to worship Him, and we just want to love people like He does."

The next day we joyfully welcomed Mary into our family. She met the One who is love itself, and we had the honor of witnessing her give her heart to Jesus. He met her, forgave her and gave her a brand-new life. Our children rejoiced and whisked her away to explore her new home.

The eyes of a little child saw and embraced the Kingdom that we adults often overlook.

The Curse of Invisibility

Can anyone see me? It is a cry heard the world over that each day I hear a little louder.

Am I worth seeing? Can you see past where I am to who I am? Will you love me enough to see behind the façade and beyond the image to what is real?

There are many ways to be invisible. I have been learning it is not just the ones discarded on rubbish dumps who are unseen. While some lives are hidden in trash heaps and slums, others are hidden behind wealth and success. But the heart cry is the same. Whether the disguise is poverty or Prada, the question remains unchanged. And so does the answer.

I have been learning to see. God has been teaching me to see both the physically poor and the truly poor as He sees them. The physically poor are the ones we have often looked past and chosen not to see. Seeing might compel us to become involved. And that involvement would surely entail risk. Risk might mean personal cost. And alas, in the culture of cost/benefit analyses, it remains easier for most of us to feign blindness and choose to live in a sightless world.

Way back when I was in university at Baylor, I was just beginning to learn to see that the world looked different through love's eyes. I was working with the homeless on the streets of Waco, Texas, and I wanted to know what it was like where they lived. I desired to identify with their pain and understand their struggles, if only in a small way.

One cold winter weekend, therefore, I decided to abandon the confines of my safe academic world for the streets. Some friends and I took only the clothes on our backs and purposed to spend that Saturday and Sunday on the streets. It was a baby step. It was a small effort to identify. It was a choice to have eyes to see.

We met with some of the homeless men who had become our friends, and they graciously invited us into their world. They were a little perplexed but welcoming.

What did it feel like to spend the night never quite asleep with harsh gravel scraping your face if you changed position? To be so cold you could barely move your lips on demand? What was it like to have to stand labeled with a sign and beg, only to have people roll up their windows, lock their doors and look away? To be reviled and run out of restaurants? Not even to be offered a drink of water? What did it feel like to walk into a church building after a week with no shower, hungry and wearing dirty clothes?

I never fully knew the answers to these questions. I always had the option to go home. But I did see a little more than I did before.

I will never forget standing with a sign at the intersection near my college dorm and having people I *knew* lock their doors and turn away. I had become invisible.

I will never forget the whisperings and the looks as we walked into a church service on Sunday morning. I had joined the ranks of the contemptible.

I will never forget D.J. (not his real name), one of my homeless friends who invited me into his world and shared with me a tortilla he had purchased from the $1.25 he had scraped together. I became rich.

I will never forget when Preacher (his street name) told us stories of riding the rails and preaching to the vagabonds. He told them about Jesus making Himself known to the lowest and the least.

I was learning who was truly poor. And it was not these people.

A few weeks later I met with my supervisor about a student internship. That day I was reeling from the blow of sudden loss. Just before entering her heated, well-guarded, beautifully accessorized office, I had found out my friend D.J. had frozen to death the night before.

Now D.J. was far from a saint. He was addicted to alcohol and caught in a downward spiral that kept him on the streets. He wanted to be free. Friends in our community had sat up nights with him as he tried to shake the tremors of addiction and find a new life free from alcohol. He never quite shook it. But he loved Jesus, and Jesus loved him. And he was our friend.

As I entered her office my supervisor began to go on and on about the homeless man she had found hiding in their church courtyard trying to take shelter from the bitter December cold. How aggravating these social nuisances were, she said. They had to change all the locks to protect the new computers in the Sunday school classrooms. I was dumbfounded. D.J. had frozen to death in the field across the street from my supervisor's church.

Her indifference was more shocking than her blindness. She spoke of him as one might speak of a cockroach.

I learned a lot that year about who the truly poor were. They were not D.J. or Preacher. They were not the ones rendered invisible by another's blindness. The truly poor were the ones like me who had lived our lives imprisoned in cushioned boxes of fear, wearing delicate disguises of the lists of successes and certificates of accomplishments we chose to let define us. Poverty and blindness are almost always first states of the heart.

When Others Turn Away

That was one of my first lessons in learning to see. In the years since then I have had many more. Seeing has been a constant challenge here in Sudan. The need is often so overwhelming that some days I would rather just turn away. But love sees. Love pays the price to see even when it hurts, even when it costs. The cost of blindness is much higher. Destinies hang in the balance.

It was nearing midnight on our first Sudanese New Year's Eve 2006. We had determined to pray and worship in the changing of the year. About twenty of us, including our first children, had gathered around a keyboard and were singing our hearts out to Jesus.

Suddenly we were interrupted by a commotion of voices outside. As it was almost 1:00 A.M., we were a little concerned for security reasons. One of the young men went out to investigate.

A few moments later he returned with an incoherent, demonized woman clothed in rags and muttering to herself. When she came near us she began to writhe as the spirits in her revealed themselves.

We all looked at one another a little unsure as to how to proceed. It would have been much easier to turn away and hide in our agenda. It would have been much easier not to see. But here she was, a dear woman for whose freedom Jesus had already paid the price. And she walked in our front door at 1:00 A.M., not knowing her name or where she had come from.

Her eyes would not focus or look at us. If we got too close she wriggled and moaned. Voices shouted lies of suicide. Death and insanity looked as though they had another victim firmly in their grasp.

But Jesus.

He led her to wander onto our compound. He brought her to our door. And here she was. Here right in front of our eyes God had given us an opportunity to see. Would we take the time? Would we take the risk? Would we dare to trust His love on behalf of another?

What would love look like to this woman? Love might as well be spelled F-R-E-E-D-O-M.

We gathered around her and worshiped, binding the demons from manifesting further or clouding her mind. I addressed the spirits that plagued her.

"In Jesus' name, you will be quiet. I bind you from speaking to her or making a fuss. You are not allowed to interfere. Shush in Jesus' name."

She settled down and stopped writhing. It really was that simple. We continued to worship until Jesus gave us the okay to continue. The stronger God's presence came, the more our guest seemed to be at peace.

Soon she was lucid, and we introduced her to Jesus. She willingly gave her life to Him. He set her free. We commanded her demonic tormentors to leave, and they did. She did not belong to them anymore. She now belonged to Jesus.

In a matter of minutes her memory returned, and she knew her name. She remembered her children. She remembered home. A mother was returned to her little ones. She went home the next day.

More than freedom was restored that night. This precious woman also received the dignity that comes when a person realizes she is worth seeing, worth loving.

When many others turn away, Jesus turns my eyes to see what He sees. He directs me to stop and ask what He is doing in the moment. It is the seeing that makes one stop.

Seeing Means Stopping

Jesus spoke of another man, the good Samaritan, who chose to see and to stop. This Scripture has long been one of my favorites.

In it I hear the call to see the Christ who comes to me in disguise and to stop. The account of the good Samaritan challenges me that I have not truly seen until I am willing to stop. It is a reminder that I will never be able to become an accurate expression of Love's heart until I learn to see through Love's eyes.

It was midday that fateful day on the Jericho road, and the sun was high. Rivulets of sweat soaked the traveler's back. He looked around him uneasily. It was a dangerous road even in broad daylight. Rumors of gangs of thieves in the area had reached the inn where he stayed last night. He picked up his pace, muttering a silent stream of prayers.

In an instant his journey changed. Out of seemingly thin air they appeared. Four men with evil snarls ripped his bag from his back. They tore his clothes off and began to beat him without mercy. Blow by blow his world began to spin and fade from view.

Sometime later he regained his awareness. Was it one hour, two hours? He did not know. Time ceased to have any meaning as pain eclipsed his ability to think. Consciousness came and went in waves. Maybe that was a strange grace.

Fear gripped his heart as he heard the sound of approaching steps on the path. He could not even move to see who was coming. Was it the thieves to finish what they had started? Or was it some gift of help? His hope soared when he saw the long, flowing robes of a priest.

A man close to God—surely he will see me. Surely he will help, thought the traveler.

The priest approached. Seeing the dying traveler on the side of the road, he quickly adjusted his step and crossed over to the

other side, casting an anxious glance around him. The priest
showed no signs of stopping.

The traveler did not even have the strength to cry out after
him as he left. Another wave of darkness blacked out his swollen vision.

More steps approached. A worship leader came into view. The
traveler recognized him from a local synagogue. This time help
had come, he was certain. But again the scenario was repeated.
The worship leader looked straight at him. *Has he even seen
me? Surely he has.* This man knew him. But he looked right in
his eyes and kept walking.

The darkness tugging at the edges of his vision was overtaken
only by the sense of despair rising in his heart. Hope was too
great an effort. He resigned himself to the inevitable.

A third person came, this time with a donkey. He heard the
clip clop of the mule's steps approaching. The traveler did not
even bother to open his eyes. If two men of God did not stop,
why should he think someone else would?

The steps slowed. Then they slowed some more. Finally they
stopped, and a shadow was cast over where he lay. A foreigner's
voice said in a distinctly Samaritan accent, "Are you okay?" The
answer was a fairly obvious no.

The traveler forced his eyes open to find himself face-to-face
with a dark-eyed stranger looking at him with grave concern.
"You are a Samaritan!" was what he tried to say. But through
his swollen, cracked lips the only sounds that came out were,
"Ur ah wa-ah-wah." A mixture of surprise and instant disdain
filled his heart.

But it was soon washed away by gratitude. This Samaritan stranger risked his life to help the traveler. He bandaged his wounds. He gave him water to drink. He put clothes on his beaten body. He took him to an inn where the traveler could recover. This Samaritan paid for his expenses out of his own pocket.

He could not believe that someone from a people so despised would be the one who saved his life. What was this love that was so much stronger than hate? He did not know, but he purposed in his heart to find out.

What a beautiful story of love Jesus told in the parable of the good Samaritan! Jesus was always pushing the envelope to make a point. So who was the face of His love? Was it the face of religion? Was it the face of devotion? Was it the face of title or position? Was it the face of success? No.

It was the face of an unknown stranger who had eyes to see the one in need and loved enough to stop.

To See His Glory

I have read many times the promise that His glory will cover the earth as the waters cover the seas (see Habakkuk 2:14). This promise has tugged at my heart and painted questions on the canvas of my imagination. *What would it look like to see God's glory so deep that the experience of it covers the earth as waters fill the seas? What would it look like to see the ash heaps of nations transformed by His love, to see the wastelands and war zones become the gardens of His promises?*

Earlier this year I was spending time in worship just before I was to share in a church service when the Lord visited me. It was one of those life-defining moments with Jesus. It was so intense that it was hard to pull out of it to preach. I am not sure I ever did. It was more as though the whole room got pulled into encountering Him with me instead.

I saw thick, deep darkness pulsating over the face of the globe. In the midst of the darkness these see-through, transparent lovers were waking up all over the planet. They were rubbing the sleep from their eyes.

The Son began to dawn in them, and because they were see-through the glory light of love began to burst forth from their innermost beings. They carried the light of His glory! They carried His dawn into the darkness! They dispelled darkness just by showing up. They had huge hearts that took up their whole chests, and their chests were on fire, literally burning and beating with His passionate love. Their gazes were fixed on the Lamb, and nothing could tear their eyes from the altogether lovely, beautiful One. Wherever they followed Him, out of their innermost beings came rivers of life and love, glory light and fire. Pulsating torrents flowed out of them until the earth began to flood with this liquid glory love.

This is the movement of love! I thought. What would happen when I became so consumed in love that I was transformed into a see-through lover of His heart? Perhaps His light would rise, His glory would radiate and His Kingdom would come in and through a life completely given over to Him. The love I saw in that visitation is not some ethereal concept. It is completely and utterly practical. And it all starts with seeing with heaven's perspective.

Soon after that encounter I went to visit one of our key leaders who was in the hospital in Uganda. After a meandering drive through the backwoods of the northern Ugandan outback—a trip through several unintended destinations, as my hired driver got lost and took me the scenic route—I arrived at my intended destination of Arua. What should have been a six-hour drive became a two-day adventure. I am grateful for African time in moments like these.

I walked up to the hospital entrance dusty and tired from the journey. The pungent stench of sickness and disease filled my nose. Listless shadows of people lined the benches and mats. Coughs and cries punctuated an eerie silence. As I made my way through the unfamiliar maze of sidewalks and wards, I noticed a small woman sitting on the ground begging. Her sightless eyes stared vacantly into the nothingness that surrounded her.

I was on a mission to see one of our leaders who was battling cancer. I felt a tug at my heart, however, and made a mental note to look for her on my way back out.

Finally I found the room I was seeking. The atmosphere was thick with pain and unanswered questions. No stranger to a hospital myself, I decided if we were all going to be in the hospital together we might as well have a party! I went and bought sodas for everyone in the room. The aunties and village mamas visiting the elderly man in the adjacent bed lit up with the thought of cold drinks.

I shared stories and testimonies as the room erupted in laughter—holy laughter that gripped them so hard they were crying. Wave upon wave of God's presence filled that little hospital room, and I had the privilege of praying for everyone there, including the random assortment of family members who came in and out.

The women there gave me my first kawkwa name: *Ajonyeh.* It means "one who is full of love." I cried. Perhaps that meant they encountered His love in our time together. If I simply live out of the love God has for me and love the one in front of me each day, then the day is successful regardless of what does or does not get accomplished.

That afternoon I said my farewells. The beggar woman who had caught my gaze earlier was nowhere to be found. I went to sleep that night with her face gently gracing my dreams.

Day two came and went without the opportunity to find her.

On the third day of my hospital visits I woke up with a prayer in my heart. *Please, Jesus, let her path cross mine today.*

I felt this overwhelming compassion bubbling inside of me. It was not a "thus saith the Lord" instruction; it was a love compulsion. She was not at the places I had seen her before. So I went searching. I took one of my friends who spoke a little of the local language, and we went on a scavenger hunt for yet another treasure, this one hidden in a hospital.

We easily found her and introduced ourselves, exchanging the customary greetings. I asked her what had happened to her eyes. She had lost her sight years ago, and all she could see was white fuzz. I found out she loved Jesus and her name was Gloria.

"Well, Gloria, my name is Michele. I was wondering if we could pray for your eyes to be healed. Jesus loves you, and He wants to heal your vision."

Yes, I realize that last statement was a bit bold, but it came out of my mouth before I quite knew what I had said. Tears welled up in her empty gaze, and she eagerly nodded.

Suffice it to say that a little white woman with one leg kneeling in the dirt together with a little blind woman trusting for a miracle—well, we were quite a pair. The spectacle drew a crowd.

I felt nothing spectacular. I did not feel extremely anointed or like the person of power for the hour. All I felt was compassion for this small Ugandan woman. I placed my hand on her eyes and commanded them to open in Jesus' name. I did not follow any particular formula or method. I just did what I saw Jesus doing in the moment. In my heart of hearts, I cried out, *Jesus, please show off Your glory here.*

She had no vision at all when we began. The surrounding crowd grew rapidly. I took my hand off her eyes, and a look of surprise crossed her face. She could see light and shadows for the first time in years. More and more people were gathering to watch the display in the dirt.

One thing I have learned in praying for healing is that when a person experiences progress of any kind, thank Jesus for what He is doing and keep praying! I continued to pray.

Soon she began describing the colors of what we wore, who was sitting, squatting or kneeling where and how many fingers I held up. At first I was not sure what to think. My Western analytical overdrive kicked into full gear. Had she really been blind? Was she simply a good guesser? Was this a show? But the tears in her now-focusing eyes and the look of awe on her face assured me that this was authentic. I still was not sure what to do. I was in a daze. Had I just seen a blind person healed? It had taken less than fifteen minutes.

The crowd began to clap and cheer and seemed equally unsure of how to respond. My mind was reeling. They looked at me, and I looked at them, and we all looked at Gloria, and she looked at us. I hugged her, got up and left, leaving a gaping crowd behind me. It did not even occur to me that preaching might be in order.

An hour later in town, a woman who had been in the crowd found me. She looked at me and said, "Honey, you forgot to preach. Most of that crowd was unreached, and they wanted to know what happened. But that's okay. Some of us explained what they had just witnessed and shared how to come to know Jesus. Many gave their lives to Him. Thought you might like to know. We got their names and will make sure they all get visits and Bibles."

God had it covered! I am glad He knows what He is doing.

It later dawned on me. Gloria. Jesus had been speaking to me about seeing His glory revealed through lives laid down in love, and the first blind person I personally saw healed in Africa was named Gloria, or Glory. I think He just might have been making a point!

In many ways I have been a lot like Gloria. I, too, needed eyes to see. I have needed Jesus to touch my vision, to transform the way I see and interact with my world. I need Him. They need Him. We need Him. Not more religion or legislation, orchestration or explanation—what we need is to live out an encounter with the One who is real, who is love, who never fails.

It is in this place of knowing Him that I can become His love encounter to the world around me. I have nothing to give apart from that. It is a call to compassion where I live in Him and He lives in me. It is there in that place of knowing His love that I can become His embrace to others. It is there, face-to-face with Him, that I, too, receive healing for my vision and learn to look at all of life through His eyes.

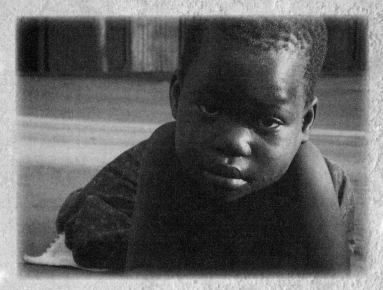

One of my greatest teachers

6 Miracles in the Mud

It was a wet afternoon. The rain had overtaken the compound yard and transformed it into a muddy river. The gate opened slightly, and a frail, elderly woman, half bent over and leaning heavily on her bamboo cane, limped onto our compound. She had two young children in tow whom she was bringing for our consideration. She sat under the slight shelter of our makeshift porch gingerly rubbing her knee as the rain continued to pelt.

About twenty minutes after they arrived, someone came to tell me we had visitors. Nothing moves fast here. The rain had abated marginally, and I picked my way through the muddy mire of our front yard. Mud and crutches usually do not mix too well.

One of our staff introduced me to *Abuba* ("Grandmother"). I looked at her weathered face with its deeply ingrained wrinkles that framed feisty eyes. Instantly I liked her.

Her eyes flashed as she told of losing her children to the war. The silent regret of a mother having to bury her babies is an all-too-common reality here. Her son had died in the war. Her daughter-in-law had left the children at the grandmother's doorstep because her new husband did not want them. I looked down at the cherub-faced children, ages eight and ten, fiddling with their clothes. Grandma obviously loved them. Her bringing them to us was a decision of last resort.

She went on to describe how difficult life in the bush was with the pain in her knee. She could not work, earn a living or even handle basic household chores, which in these parts does not mean unloading the dishwasher or tossing a quick load into the laundry machine. *Basic chores* means what most of us would consider a full day of manual labor: walking two miles to find water, pumping the water into twenty-liter plastic cans (I cannot even lift one of these, let alone carry it!) and carrying them back on your head, washing the family's clothes by hand, gathering firewood and cooking a meager meal over an open fire, tilling the family garden and so on. My heart went out to her.

These children belonged with their grandma. They had already lost enough. I felt a nudge in my spirit to pray for her knee.

So I asked her, "Abuba, may I pray for Jesus to heal your knee? Then you can take the children home with you and be able to care for them yourself." Her eyes turned soft, and she willingly nodded.

I knelt down in the mud in our little front yard and placed my hand on her knee. I commanded it to be made whole in Jesus' name. I asked the Holy Spirit to come and fill her and remove every pain in her body. It was a simple prayer. It was a prayer one of my five-year-olds could have prayed. It took about two minutes.

I looked at her, and her expression had not changed. She had stared open-eyed at me the whole time. There was no "receiving" posture, as in many places in the West. She just waited and watched as I prayed. Jesus whispered into my spirit, *Have her test it.*

So often it seems that the testing of a healing releases its fullness. I stood up from the mud that now coated the bottom half of my skirt. She looked at me and "tsk-tsked" me for getting dirty on her behalf. I motioned for her to stand up and bend her knee. *"Abuba, keif intum? Giwaja kalaas?"* ("Grandma, how are you? Is the pain gone?")

She stood up and began to stamp the ground with her foot. Then she began to squat up and down. A look of relief and joy filled her face, and she began to laugh almost incredulously. Then she began to dance. Her knee was completely healed. She did not need to say a word; her face and actions said it all.

She grabbed me in a hug and handed me her bamboo cane. With the step of someone half her age, she took her grandchildren in hand and with a final *shukran* ("thank you") disappeared through the gate.

I stood there holding her bamboo stick, watching her leave. It still adorns a corner of my room. It serves as a reminder to me of the supernatural realm that God desires to be interwoven into our everyday goings-on of life. These miracles are not reserved only for a select, anointed few. These are simple miracles of childlike faith that happen in the mud all around us as we learn to live in God's heart of love.

Soccer Balls from Heaven

"Mama, Mama, Mama, *nina deru* footballs." ("We want foot-balls.")

"*Aye, ana arif itakum deru* footballs." ("Yes, I know you guys want footballs.")

At that point in time, however, I could not give footballs (soccer balls) to them. It was not that I did not want to give them footballs. We just did not have the money for it. We barely had enough money for food. I did not have the ability to give them this desire of their hearts. But I knew Someone who did!

So we embarked on an evening ritual of sorts. For three weeks my boys came up to me every day asking for footballs. About four in the afternoon a small group headed by one of our older boys would come knocking on my door. "Mama, we want footballs."

Again I would explain that I could not give them footballs but that I wanted them to have footballs, too. They would smile. I would suggest, "Let's stop and ask Papa for footballs." (*Papa* is my term of endearment for our Father God. He is our Papa in heaven. You might call it my personal, contemporary English version of the Hebrew word *Abba*.)

"I cannot give them to you right now, but He can."

So diligently every day, afternoon and evening, a concerted prayer effort for footballs swept the compound. I marveled as

I watched God's hand in motion. There was something much bigger at play than a potential game of football.

Our part of Africa has no postal service or banking infrastructure. If we want to collect our mail or withdraw necessary funds, we must embark upon an eight-hour trip to Uganda over unpaved, often inaccessible roads plagued with regional instabilities. It was time for another trip, and I just hoped that the transfer of funds would be there to greet me. Our family had enough food for three days. It would take me one day to travel, one day to do the business needed and one day to return. I was cutting it close.

I left a friend who was visiting us at the time to oversee the compound in my absence. I waved good-bye as I walked out of the gate to the bus stop in the pre-dawn light. Soon I was bouncing on my way, surrounded by goats and chickens, the only Westerner for miles. As the large metal monster creaked and groaned its way closer to the city where our bank is located, I prayed, "Jesus, please take care of my kids. Please let the money be there."

Eight hours later we rolled into the dusty border town of Arua that is our nearest contact with the outside fiscal world. I found a room at a local guesthouse and fell into a dreamless sleep.

The next morning I made my way to the bank. My heart sank when I realized the transfer had not arrived yet. We had such a close window of time. *Jesus, please do something!* I sent word to the compound that I was delayed, and my prayers were echoed back home as food began to dwindle. Even if the money came the next day, it would be another two days before I reached home.

On day three the mamas cooked the last food in the store-room. We could only wait to see what God would do. A virtual world away from my children, I was completely helpless and could do nothing but pray.

That day the money did come, but I could not get back any sooner than the following evening. Pictures of my children hungry ran through my mind's eye. *Jesus, help.*

When I arrived home the following day I was unsure of what I would find. Having not eaten in almost two days, would the children be crying out from hunger? Would the staff be upset? Would the visitors be on the next plane out? I did not know.

I honestly did not expect what I found. I was greeted by beaming faces and excited voices bubbling over to tell me the story of what God had done. I should have known the heart of our Papa in heaven better!

The day before at lunchtime they had cooked and eaten the last food in the house. As dinnertime neared the children began to pray. Not long afterward a truck honked at our gate. At that time our ministry was less than two months old, and no one knew we were there. Yet into our compound pulled a pickup truck filled with USAID food and supplies, and the driver asked for us by name.

Our visiting friend was skeptical at first. She informed them clearly that we had no money with which to pay them.

"No, no, you do not understand. Your compound is on our distribution list. We just need your signature. We have to deliver this food to you." Amid shouts of joy from our family, the USAID men began to offload basins of beans and rice and sugar. Dinner was served! And it only got better.

One of the men stood on the back of the truck and quieted the cheering crowd. "We heard you had kids here and thought you might have a use for these . . ."

He pulled out a huge sack of—you guessed it—soccer balls. Our kids began to jump, dance and clap, shrieking with delight.

"Wait, wait . . . If you like these," he said as he held up the soccer balls, "then we thought you might also like these." With that, he held up a second sack overflowing with soccer jerseys. The squeals of glee might have been heard clear up to Juba!

I arrived home to find my children eating their favorite meal of beans and rice, playing a game of football in the mud and wearing their new soccer jerseys. Indeed there was something much bigger at play!

Jesus was strengthening my faith. He was proving to me that He really would take care of our little family. He was showing us all that He is concerned with not just our basic needs but our deepest heart desires as well. That still undoes me.

Our children have never forgotten how Papa fed them and brought them soccer balls from heaven. Neither have I. In His Kingdom, there is truly more than enough.

Ania Smiles

I have been privileged to witness the blind see and the deaf hear. But honestly some of the greatest miracles I have witnessed are the ones when the hearts of our children are healed by the power of God's love. The transformation of their little hearts from shattered, traumatized and rejected to loved, restored and cherished is something only heaven could bring to pass.

Ania's (not her real name) story was a miracle that happened quite literally in the mud. From this little girl I have learned more about God's extravagant grace and persistent compassion than I have from any other person in my life to date.

Ania came to us at three and a half years old with her two brothers. She was a shadow of a little girl. She refused to play. She would not let anyone touch her. She had radar for the dirtiest, filthiest place on the compound. She would find it, lie down in the dirt and wail for hours.

If someone tried to pick her up, she would scratch, flail and head straight back to the filth as soon as they let her go. Most of the mamas gave up trying and let her lie on the ground and cry. Her cries were especially haunting.

Often I wondered how many times before she had cried like that and no one heard her or came to her. She had the epitome of an orphan spirit. She was sure that no one would love her or want her, and to prove her point she made it as difficult as possible for us.

Papa, what do I do? How do I love her? Immediately a passage from Philippians 2 came to mind:

> Your attitude should be the same as that of Christ Jesus: who, being in very nature God, did not consider equality with God something to be grasped, but made himself nothing, taking the very nature of a servant, being made in human likeness.

> verses 5–7

Jesus came where I am. I must therefore go where Ania is.

So I did. I found her lying in the mud, and I lay down right beside her. I did not touch her or talk to her. I did not look at her, for I knew that would only make her wail louder. I simply lay down with her. She knew I was there. I was just *there*. The next day I lay down beside her in the same manner, but this time I put my hand out in view. Nothing seemed to happen. Refusing to be discouraged, I tried again. The next time I found her I again lay down and put out my hand. This time her small hand found its way into mine. Slowly we got up together, only to have that scene repeated over and over again throughout the following weeks.

Slowly, almost imperceptibly, a miracle was happening in Ania's heart. She began to realize that she was loved and safe and wanted. She was worth getting dirty for. She was worth looking foolish for. She was worthy of love. She was not alone or abandoned. Her cries no longer echoed unheard in the silence.

I will never forget when I saw Ania smile for the first time. I burst into tears. I could not help it.

Now she is five, and she smiles a lot. She curls up in my lap and loves to help our younger children. The other day she broke up a brewing fight. She plays and laughs and loves to be hugged.

Ania is no longer an orphan. She has come home.

Journeying with her has taught me about the richness of Papa's grace. He did not tell me to get up out of the dirt of my own pain and shame. He did not ask me to get it all together and then let Him know when I was ready to shape up. No. He lay down in the mud with me. He put out His hand and just waited—for me to see, for me to trust, for me to put my hand in His and for us to stand up together.

I understand Ania. The only difference between us is that while her pain was evident, mine was hidden inside my heart.

God's love is big. He comes and finds us in the muddy places of our deepest hurts and darkest closets. He loves us so much that He moves heaven and earth to show us His extravagant grace. He loves us so much that He embraces us even in the mud. And He loves us too much to leave us there.

Tourists from Another Realm

God wants His supernatural realm to become our normal, everyday reality. He wants to bring us miracles in the mud. I am sure of that because of how specifically He watches out for our needs—and our desires. Just look at the soccer ball scenario. He always waits to prove Himself real and strong on our behalf. Sometimes, however, I do not have eyes to see what He is doing in the moment. In the middle of caring for children, meeting needs and running a ministry, it can be easy enough to miss.

One morning one of our short-term volunteers and I had a powerful time with Jesus. As we spent time in prayer together, Jesus showed us a warehouse in heaven that is filled with different body parts. Eyeballs were blinking on a shelf. Lungs were inhaling in a corner. Bones were neatly organized in rows.

Yes, I agree, that sounds incredibly strange. It was indeed a tad on the sci-fi side. But since Jesus died and paid the price for our healing, it makes sense that He would have a room in heaven filled with what we need.

A little later that day the volunteer and I decided to go check email. The Internet café was a half-mile trek down a road on which even heavy-duty vehicles went only five miles an hour to keep from flipping.

We were walking on the muddy road and chatting about the things Jesus was showing us when a truck pulled up, seemingly out of nowhere. The whole scenario should have struck me as odd right away, but it did not. In front of us was an old Land Rover–esque delivery-type truck with safari memorabilia fixed to its patchwork rainbow paint job. It was driven by two very white, blond, European-looking men.

"Hi, guys, what organization are you with?" I asked nonchalantly. No one comes to our parts unless they are affiliated with an organization of some sort.

They hesitated and then smiled. "We are . . . well . . . tourists!"

"Wow, tourists? Where are you going?"

"Cameroon and Central African Republic. What do you do here?"

"We have a children's home. That is our gate over there." While I talked with them, my friend was peeking in the windows, thinking how strange it was that their truck appeared to be completely empty. She saw no luggage, no water, no food, not even a map! Yet the truck was actually there in the natural. It was there. I leaned on it.

"Which way is Maridi?" they asked. Maridi is a city to our west.

"Go to the end of the road, turn left, then go straight for nine hours. God bless!"

I waved them off in the right direction, and my visiting friend and I kept walking. I looked back over my shoulder not a minute later, and the truck had vanished. *Hmmm. That is odd. Oh, well.*

"Wow, tourists in Sudan," I said. "Who would have thought?"

"Michele . . . don't you think that was a little strange?"

"Well, now that you mention it, I guess so."

"Try tourists from another realm! You really were entertaining angels unaware. I think they missed the how-to-blend-in-on-earth class!" We wondered about the encounter but then continued with our day, which went on without further angelic incident—and without any million-dollar pledges in my inbox.

Back at home that evening we began our favorite pastime of telling God-stories. With only one, lone, intrepid short-term volunteer and me to oversee our growing Sudanese family and with only one kerosene light, what else were we to do at night?

In the middle of our storytelling session God opened my spiritual eyes to see a myriad of angels step through the walls into the small room. That night I did not see them with my natural eyes. What I saw was with the eyes of my spirit. They were translucent forms superimposed on the room around me. God's presence began to grow stronger and stronger. Then one angel stepped forward with a huge grin and held out a spinal column.

I needed a spine, too, but I saw that this one was for a person much taller than I. So I looked at my friend and asked, "Honey, you don't by any chance need a spine, do you?"

Surprised, she replied, "Why, yes, I do. I have battled with scoliosis and am often in pain."

"Well, I just saw an angel walk into the room carrying one that looks to be about your size. Maybe we should pray."

I placed my hand on her back and immediately felt as if an electric current magnetized it there. God's glory came so strongly that she was unable to sit up and slid off the bed to the floor, still with my hand glued to her back. It was not convenient. It was not comfortable. But it was God.

Waves and waves of current flowed down my arm through my hand. As she lay immobilized by God's presence, I saw the angel place the spine on her back, and it dissolved into place. My hand was stuck to her back for almost four hours. Then she got up and went to bed. I did the same, thinking, *Wow, what a day!*

The next morning I opened my eyes to see my friend about three inches taller than she had been. "Whoa, check your back!" It was straight, and she had absolutely no pain.

Then it dawned on me. One heavenly visitation to the body parts room the morning before. One angelic encounter with a "delivery" truck on the muddy roadside in the afternoon. One supernatural delivery of a spine! It all went together and made a kind of otherworldly sense. Yet in the moment it felt completely and totally normal. Perhaps that was because it was supposed to be.

On the Road Again

The fact that we must drive across risky territory to a neighboring country in order to get our mail and to handle even basic financial transactions definitely keeps life interesting. The road we travel is frequented by what the United Nations calls OAGs, or Other Armed Groups. It can be especially treacherous after dark.

I was returning with some of our leaders from one such trip in our ancient Land Rover, "Lemonade." (Remember our experiment in the power of prayer and the efficacy of duct tape?) We had been delayed by road conditions and reached the border of Uganda and Sudan at sundown. We still faced what should have been a five- to six-hour journey on a normal day. But with the impending night and the fact that the road was a mud bog, we were looking at potentially seven to eight hours across volatile territory in the dark. And on this particular trip we were carrying more resources than usual because of several projects in full swing. *Help us, Jesus.*

A common trick of armed groups here is to park cars across the road simulating an accident, effectively forming a barricade. When vehicles are forced to slow down, the men jump out with guns loaded.

It was not too long until the faint headlight beam illuminated a line of parked cars across the road. None of them were running. They were not moving but were set in place in the growing muddy mess. Danger was tangible, and we could feel fear try to wrap its suffocating grasp around our hearts.

What does one do in the face of a likely ambush? We decided to try worship. It seemed to work for David.

We all simultaneously broke out into a chorus of praise and began to pray in the Spirit. Just as we were about to switch gears to slow down, the impossible happened before our eyes. It was as if a huge invisible hand came down between the end car and its nearest neighbor, pushing it horizontally out of the way. We drove right through without incident.

After our miracle of protection, we really began to worship and praised God throughout the rest of the trip. Before we knew it we were driving up to the gate of Yei. I thought, *Wow, time flies when you are enjoying Jesus!*

As our truck bounced its way up to our compound gate a few moments later I wondered, *Why are the kids still up and the lights on?* Our compound was on generator power for only two hours a day, from 7:00 to 9:00 P.M. I wondered why they all were up so late and the generator was still on. Then I glanced down at my watch. We had started this minimum six-hour journey at 6:00 P.M. It was only 8:15. Our six-hour journey had been completed in less than two and a half hours!

What lesson did I learn from this encounter? Perhaps that God is much bigger and better than I give Him credit. He is better than I believe and kinder than I conceive. He is bigger than armed ambushes, financial meltdowns and broken hearts. Even when the road we travel looks like a quagmire of obstacles, Papa is bigger than them all. We can trust Him even in the middle of the darkest parts of our journey. If need be, He will even reach down from heaven to move the things that try to block us from bringing the reality of His Kingdom into the places of our human impossibilities.

Light of the Father

Our days have settled into a fairly normal routine. Living with us in our house are eighty children who wake in the morning to do chores and eat breakfast. (We care for many more children off compound as well.) Then the older children go off to school.

Our younger children up to third grade join about two hundred more "scholars," as they are called here, from the community in our school on the compound. We call it the Dream School, for we want our children to learn how to dream God's dreams for them. The afternoons are filled with lunch, homework, playtime and a few more chores. Bath time is followed by dinner and evening worship. Then the children are tucked in and sent off to the land of sweet Jesus dreams with love and hugs. Our day is simply a family dynamic played out on a large scale.

I share this Kingdom adventure with a small army of 23 full-time Sudanese staff, a growing missionary team and a constant stream of visitors. In our muddy, everyday normality of ups and downs and highs and lows, our ministry team has been learning to embrace and expect the supernatural reality of God's love to transform the mundane with the miraculous. In this place and with this family, Papa speaks to us about carrying His light into the darkness.

I awoke one morning, and Jesus whispered into my heart that He was bringing us a special baby girl soon whose arrival would speak to me of things that were on His heart. I was elated because all my baby girls at that time were rapidly becoming rambunctious toddlers—and because I love knowing more the heart of my Jesus.

A few days later a silent man in worn fatigues came and sat along our bamboo fence waiting for me. Holding a moving bundle, he asked if we could take his infant daughter to live with us.

"I went to the other children's homes. They would not even look at her. They had no space. I am afraid she might die if no one helps her. You are my last option. Everyone says you will take any child brought to you. You love our people and do not turn anyone away who really needs help."

I asked what had happened.

"My wife hung herself two nights ago. The pain was too much for her." Tears welled up in my eyes as I watched the grieved face of this father recount the full story. The mother had suffered a complication while giving birth. It took six months and a two-day trek to a special hospital in Congo to get to the root of the problem. By the time they discovered the cause, it was too late. Her uterus was rotting inside of her, and she was told she would die. So she walked 75 miles from the hospital in Congo in excruciating pain to bring her little girl home to a village near Yei, and then she committed suicide. The father was a disabled soldier who had no way to care for his baby. The mother had no living relatives, and her father's family refused even to see the child. For me to send her away would be to give her a death sentence.

"Of course she can come live with us." Where we would put her remained to be seen. But if need be, she would sleep with me. He laid her in my arms, and I looked into her small shining face. Yet another promise from heaven.

"What is the baby's name?" I asked, smiling the goofy grin that always crosses my face when I see a precious baby.

"Noora Aba." Light of the Father. I was stunned. Here she was. The little girl Jesus told me was coming.

Her eyes looked up and locked with mine. It was uncanny. It was as if she knew her heavenly Papa had brought her home and she was safe. She giggled a quiet little laugh, nestled into

LOVE HAS A FACE

my arms and fell asleep as though she belonged there. And she did. She was my personal reminder that in the middle of the darkest of situations, the light of our Father's love shines brighter still. She was helping me to learn that regardless of the road that leads me to His arms, I am safe in the Father's love and at home in His heart.

Child's Play

The night before an outreach in a small village, our kids and I were hanging out after evening prayers just laughing and being silly in our courtyard. Ten-year-old Viola, another of our miracles, grabbed a tree branch from the ground. She turned it into a makeshift microphone and started speaking in her best preacher's voice. Her imitation was so powerful that I asked her to preach at the outreach the next day.

Amidst her giggles she shyly agreed. "What do I say, Mama?"

"What you just shared was awesome, but whatever Jesus puts on your heart to tell people about His love is what you say."

So preach she did. The next day we took our team of older children to the village. It was a small crowd—about fifteen people in all. Here are the words from Viola's first sermon:

Alleluia. We are ready to hear the word of the Lord.

If you are here, Jesus wants to heal you. If you are not here, Jesus still wants to heal you. He will heal the blind and open the ears of the deaf today.

He loves you and wants you to know that stealing is bad and so is poisoning people. Amen.

MIRACLES IN THE MUD

The crowd was enraptured. They had never seen anything like it. A little girl who had been abandoned stood in authority before them as a daughter of the King of kings, powerfully sharing the reality of God's Kingdom. Half the crowd came forward to receive Jesus. Several were healed of various infirmities.

As I watched my Viola radiate His presence, I realized once again that shining His light and seeing His love break loose can be as simple as child's play. Learning to recognize everyday miracles and unexpected encounters just might lead us into a life lived on earth as it is in heaven.

Yes, God desires that His supernatural realm be interwoven into our everyday lives. His miracles are for all of us, everywhere, even in the far reaches of southern Africa in the middle of the mud. All it takes is simple, childlike faith that lives in the heart of God's love.

Miracles in the mud

7 Finding Home

It was still early in the morning. The full force of the day's 120-degree heat had yet to set in. I decided to make a morning run to the market while it was less than blistering out. Actually it would be more like an early morning stroll. The children were just beginning to stir, and the compound was still relatively quiet.

I slipped through the large, blue, tin double doors that hung precariously off wooden posts to form our front gate. I looked across the mounds and precipices that formed the road. Then I saw them.

A pair of young teenagers with an elderly grandmother sat in stoic stillness in the coolness of the shade of our fence. As greetings are important in our culture, I bent down to shake their hands and offer my hello.

"Can you help us?" the young man asked.

Telling them that I was just on my way to the market would not work in this context. Sometimes love is inconvenient and interrupts your morning plans.

"What can I do for you?"

The fifteen-year-old boy looked intently into my eyes. I looked back into his and saw a young man much older than his years peering into my soul. He introduced himself as Elijah (not his real name). He went on to explain that he and his sister had lost their father and were living with a grandmother who could not care for them. If they had to return to the village they could not continue their schooling.

Thousands of children in Sudan cannot attend school. Our home exists for the worst-case scenarios, and I saw no apparent risk to the safety of these children. According to my thought process, they were not in immediate jeopardy and did not qualify for our home. But God had different thoughts on the matter.

They saw my hesitancy, and tears sprang to their eyes at the thought of being resigned to the village and no education. Elijah's younger sister, Beth (not her real name), handed me a dog-eared, faded photo of their father's funeral. A younger version of the two in front of me stared out from the picture, their faces flat and expressionless, their eyes filled with grief.

Papa, what are You doing? I silently prayed.

Take them in. They are to be part of your family, and they will be a great blessing, was His answer.

I asked them what they wanted to be when they grew up. Beth wanted to be a nurse. Elijah said he hoped to become a doctor and pastor. I saw destiny written on their lives. So I said, "Yes. Welcome home."

Even when something does not fit our criteria, even when we think we do not have any more room, even when it does not go with our plan, love makes a home. We must then throw out our plans and limits and yield to His limitless love.

Later that week I was on my way to see about parts for repairing our delinquent generator. As I picked my way through the uneven terrain, I spotted a swatch of fabric on the side of the road just by our gate. It was a small scarf of deep purple with gold embroidery that looked as if it would be more at home in India than here. I have no idea where it came from. It was definitely not native to Sudan. It was filthy and matted.

Jesus told me to pick it up and take it home. He wanted to show me something.

What? You have got to be kidding. Are You sure? Well, okay then.

This was not completely out of the ordinary, as God often speaks to me through simple things in the middle of my everyday life. Yet questions ran through my head. Could it be salvaged? Why did it catch my gaze? Was it even worth the effort? What was Jesus trying to show me?

When I got home I took the mangled fabric and soaked it overnight in washing powder and water. I then scrubbed it and set it out to dry. In the space of less than 24 hours it was transformed into something beautiful, displaying colors of royalty.

As I looked at it glistening in the sunshine the following morning, I knew I was looking at an object lesson from heaven. The smiling faces of Elijah and Beth entered my mind. Beth had become our worship leader and Elijah a cherished big brother for our children. They truly were a princess and a prince of their Papa in heaven.

Love has eyes to see royalty along the roadside and glory hidden in the unexpected gutters of life. Jesus desires the destinies of those who have been trampled and tossed aside to be restored to their full beauty. His love washes us clean, and His grace makes us new. He calls each of us in from the roadsides of life to come home to His heart. And until we find our place in His heart, we will never truly be at home.

Papa's Place

Moving to Sudan has been an opportunity for me to learn at deeper levels the reality of the Kingdom in my own life. One of my greatest lessons has been discovering more about the heart of God as *my* Papa. In my head, I always believed in Him as my Father in a generic sense, but recently my heart has begun to embrace what it means to be His daughter who is simply loved.

A few weeks after arriving in Yei, I found myself in way over my head with building estimates, quotes and details. I do not do numbers. Math was my worst subject in school. Furthermore, the building God had provided for us to rent defined *fixer-upper*, and I had never before renovated anything larger than a small bedside table. Suddenly I was swimming in numbers and projects in a foreign culture and language. How I wished my earthly dad could have zipped over from Florida to manhandle it into a semi-livable state. He can fix anything! I, on the other hand, have managed only to do myself bodily harm with a hammer.

I looked at the crumbling walls, the hideous yellow peeling paint, the filthy floors, the lack of running water and electricity, and I just about cried. I had signed the lease in faith. I did not even have money to make the down payment, let alone pay the rent and fix the place. I hired our first contractor in faith as well. Soon the bills came flooding in.

I woke up one day feeling completely overwhelmed. Had I bitten off more than I could handle? Had I missed it somewhere? A one-word prayer escaped my lips. "Help."

I rolled out of bed in the dimly lit mud hut I was renting at the time. I took my iPod and journal to the window and decided to spend the morning with Jesus. Yet the only prayer I could summon was still, "Help."

He did. He reminded me why I was wading through a bog of details that stretched my faith and patience almost to a breaking point. Soon we would open our doors (once we reattached them to the building, that is) and fill those rooms with the children He brought to us.

How clear it became! Décor was on my mind, so Jesus met me right where I was! He showed me a vision of long hallways with beautifully furnished rooms, each distinctively decorated and waiting for its occupants. Every doorway and room called out, longing for the ones for whom they were created. His attention to detail was meticulous. Each room was furnished not with mere functionality, but with what God knew its occupant would most enjoy!

I looked around at my sparse mud hut and laughed. The contrast could not have been greater. But I got the point. He reminded me that in the same way we were preparing a house, Papa had prepared His place, too! I was longing for our house to be ready and filled with orphaned and abandoned children. I was longing for them to discover that they were actually chosen

LOVE HAS A FACE

and adopted as dearly loved sons and daughters. If I was longing for these children I had not yet met, then how much more
did our Father long for us? The longing for His house to be full
pulsates with every beat of His heart.

In His Kingdom no one is turned away, and no one is left
outside. No one is left to wonder if they belong. His love finds
us on the roadside and brings us home to become royalty in
His house.

I would not invite the children I was gathering to come
home to a place with holes in the roof and rats nibbling at
their toes. I would not send them to filthy, unfurnished rooms.
I would not invite them home only to hand them a mop and
bucket and tell them to clean their own rooms, build their own
beds and find their own food. No. I was actively preparing
night and day to paint and clean and build and furnish the
house with all they needed. I did not want these children to
come and feel as though they had to earn the right to live in
the house. I wanted them to know they had the right to be in
our house because we invited them to be part of our family.
We invited them to come home.

Tears began to stream silently down my face as a greater
understanding of my Father's love for me grew in my heart. It
dawned on me that I had in the deepest part of my heart mis-
understood what it means to come to His house.

Part of my heart still felt and acted like an orphan. I did not
truly believe I was created simply to be loved as a daughter by
my Papa in heaven. I had felt it was too good to be true that
Papa loved me just because He loved me. I was busy looking for
strings and expecting the unspoken catch to emerge. Deep down

I did not really believe He wanted me to live in His house, so I was constantly trying to prove myself and earn the right to be there. I felt that if I worked hard and performed well enough, I would be accepted. If I did not, I just might wind up back on a roadside somewhere.

And suddenly here I was in the middle of the African bush. Here I was scouring the countryside looking for children who needed to live with us, and I still had remnants of orphan thinking in my own heart. I was a little girl who needed to know that she, too, was welcome and safe in Papa's arms. I had not been invited to His house just to pick up a broom and be put to work. I did not have to be good enough to earn my keep. Papa began that morning to show me the place He had prepared for me as His daughter. I was worth dying for. Is there any question that all He is and all He has is mine?

In His total kindness, God allowed me to come to an impasse in my journey so that He could bring a greater level of freedom to my heart. I realized that because I was not fully at home in His house, I was struggling to believe He wanted to make His home in ours.

An unspoken weight of worry was pressing down on me. I would have never said it at the time, but it was there. Where would the funds come from? How would it all happen? What if I failed and fell flat on my face? As I tried to make the whirling in my brain stop, Jesus dropped a verse from John into my mental fray: "My Father will love him, and we will come to him and make our home with him" (John 14:23).

Really, Papa? If You and Jesus are moving in with us, then I guess You have our needs covered, right? The heaviness of having to figure it all out lifted just a fraction as I thought about this truth.

I was preparing a place for His children to live. The doors were being attached to their hinges, the floors cleaned, the walls painted. It was His promise from heaven into which we were stepping—His promise that a place would be made ready to welcome each child He brought us, His promise of home.

Because He Loves Us

Simon and Steven (not their real names) are rascals. They are also really great teachers. These two little guys have taught me a lot about the face of God's love and the heart of our Father.

One desperately hot day not too long after we first opened our doors, an older man came to visit. Wearing a tattered shirt that almost looked as though it had a clerical collar, he had his two sons in tow. Their mother had gone insane, and he was unable to care for them.

I looked at the six- and ten-year-old boys before me. Fear and shame were etched into their eyes. Both of them were wearing rags that looked as though they would disintegrate if you so much as touched them. Their minds seemed to be held captive in the grips of hidden darkness. What would it mean to love them as Jesus did? I knew they were to move in with us and come home.

As the days and weeks progressed we learned much more of their story. Shortly before coming to us, Steven had been disrespectful to a caregiver, and that person put burning meat from the fire directly into his mouth. It was held there until Steven's mouth was seared. He could not eat or speak for weeks. He was regularly beaten and lived in constant terror. He did not know what a safe place felt like.

Steven began to show signs of serious anger issues and started acting out and fighting. In the sweltering afternoon heat one day I went to talk with him and decide what to do. I saw haunting dread in his eyes as he flinched away from my gaze.

Steven was seated in a blue plastic chair just behind our mud hut kitchen. His head was down, and he refused to look at me. He wore the expression of someone expecting great pain. I stooped down lower than he was and looked into his eyes. He had hit one of the other boys, and while this needed to be addressed I knew it was not the time.

I peered into his face and said, "Steven, I love you. You are loved. I love you because I love you. God loves you. He is not going to hurt you. We love you. We love you." Over and over again I said it until his eyes melted into puddles of tears that soaked my shoulder as I held him.

That afternoon, as I explained the love of Jesus, Steven gave his life to the One who will never hurt or abuse him. He met the only perfect Papa there ever was, is or will be. He began learning that he, too, was welcome in Papa's house by seeing that he was loved and at home in ours.

Why did I love Steven? Why was he welcome and wanted? Was it because he was the best behaved and the brightest achiever? Was it because he was incredibly gifted, with a budding international ministry? Not at all. I loved Steven because I loved him with the love of Jesus. Period.

Steven has been another step in my learning about God's unfathomable love. God loves me because He loves me. Until I really understood that I still felt like an orphan, even in Papa's house. But as my heart laid hold of more of His unconditional love, finding home became only a heartbeat away.

Victory Dances and Marshmallow Roasts

We have a lot of fun in our family. We are not all serious and somber. We love to laugh, and some of our everyday world is really humorous. This place in Papa's heart has been one of great joy.

In our first month or so of operations, a visitor brought us several bags of marshmallows. Our children had never seen or tasted anything like that before. One night we made a fire in our front yard. We grabbed a poker and the marshmallows and went to town. High-pitched giggles reverberated throughout the compound as our family enjoyed its first marshmallow roast. It was an instant hit.

Several months later a new supply of marshmallows was delivered, and we decided to have another impromptu marshmallow party. Our kids began to shout in anticipation of the gooey white sweetness that awaited them. What I did not take into account were the eight visitors staying on our compound at the time.

We were in the middle of running a discipleship course, and eight soldiers from the southern Sudanese military were living and studying with us. This discipleship class was a bit of a holy experiment: What would happen if you put together thirty people from differing tribes and denominations, some of which did not like each other, and taught them about love and the Kingdom?

Each morning and afternoon for two and a half weeks, 22 local students joined the out-of-towners who were staying with us for a real-life journey into the heart of our King. Together we had to face our fears and pain to choose forgiveness and freedom. Jesus came and showed us that we were to be like the woven grass mats we use here. The strands of our tribes and church expressions were to be woven together, over and under, to become a demonstration of His beauty in the earth. We were never to lose who we are, but in love and honor our uniquenesses were to be woven together with other's differences, allowing God to make something much greater than we could ever be in ourselves alone. It was a precious time of learning how to love and live in a Kingdom bigger than all of us.

Our children eagerly pressed around the fire, all wanting their special treat. Our military observers assessed the situation from a safe distance.

"Mama, they are eating fire," they said to me. How do you explain a blazing marshmallow to someone who has never seen one before?

"Well, it is more like soft sweets that you heat up. They are squishy and sugary on the inside. You might like the taste. Why don't you try one?"

A fleeting look of concern indicated that this was a fearful proposition. The unknown can be a scary thing in any culture. But our tall warrior friends were not to be shown up by our three-year-olds. If our children could conquer the flaming white puff, so could they. Provoked by our fearless children, they embraced the challenge one by one.

I will never forget the looks on these soldiers' faces as we handed them the fiery balls of fluff to blow out. As our first guest made the plunge into the great unknown, he positioned his mouth carefully so that only his front teeth touched the marshmallow, tentatively nibbling the smallest bite he could manage. Our kids were consumed with hilarity at his expression.

"Mmmmm," he said in relief after a few seconds, "tastes like banana. It's good." He popped the remaining marshmallow in his mouth and asked for seconds. The rest of our visitors followed suit. It was not exactly trial by fire, but almost.

Our children began to beat out familiar rhythms on our plastic jerry cans and sing their hearts out to Jesus. Worship was punctuated that night by our visiting soldiers celebrating their edible victory with majestic, twirling, tribal dance leaps around the fire. It was a sight that is forever etched on my memory: little children, village mamas and great big soldiers all dancing and spinning and beginning to find who they were in His heart.

Who is afraid of a marshmallow? Seriously? But some fears with which I struggle look equally ridiculous when I realize that I am loved and am seated in Papa's lap. It is all a matter of perspective. If I let it, fear can keep me from tasting the goodness of our God and finding my home in Him. Fear can make marshmallows into monsters. But in His love, it has no place to operate.

That night one of our local students went home to lead a neighbor witch doctor to Jesus. This young man looked past his fear and saw the heart of Jesus. God allowed him to extract the precious from the worthless and be His spokesman. Perfect love truly does drive out all fear.

Once again little children showed the way to freedom and the heart of the Father. It was they who pointed the way home.

Washed Away

Our home is always open and often has an assortment of unexpected visitors. One afternoon a friend from the Mundari tribe to our north came to visit unannounced. He brought his wife, his baby and a young girl from their village with him.

It had been a long, three-day journey. They came all that way to bring to us Michal (not her real name), a sweet, spirited teenager. She had an incurable rare skin disease, and the doctors said there was no hope. They knew we prayed for healing, so they came in faith.

Her eyes were listless. Her skin was covered with pockmarks and sores from a severe, rare kind of scabies that had progressed so violently that it was attacking her internal organs. She was in great pain. Her condition rivaled some of the cases of leprosy I had seen in India.

Immediately we prayed. There was no visible change. We invited them to stay for several days as we continued to trust Jesus for her healing. Michal spent the first two days curled up on a mat in agony. The second night she was seated on a step in our courtyard. I went over to her, put my arm around her and held her.

A year ago I would have given up. It is difficult to pray and not see an immediate miracle, especially if it means watching someone suffer. But through times of contending without seeing visible breakthrough, God had been teaching me: *Beloved, your job is to love. My job is to heal.* Instead of asking only what it would take to see a miracle transpire, I was learning also to ask, *Papa, how can I love this person like You do?*

My heart was overwhelmed with compassion. As I held Michal, everything in me wanted her to know the Jesus who is life and healing. I asked her if she had met Him before. She looked surprised. "No, Mama," she said with a wide-eyed innocence that was priceless.

"Sweetheart, He loves you. Jesus came to earth to show us how much God loves us. He paid the price of every wrong thing we have ever done. He wants to heal you. Would you like to know Him?"

Heaven invaded our little dirt yard that night as Michal gave her life to Him. I went on to tell her about Papa's house and more about His love for her. In the middle of it all, God gave me the mental image of Naaman the leper, who was healed as he bathed in the Jordan River.

Jesus whispered, *Baptize her, and she will be healed.*

I explained about water baptism, and she willingly agreed. The following day an entourage of our children went to the brackish pond in which we baptize. How disease-contaminated, leech-infested waters would be helpful for a skin disorder I was not sure. But God is God, and I am not! Michal was fully immersed. Standing there willfully ignoring whatever was slithering around my leg, I again prayed a simple prayer of faith for her healing as she re-emerged from the water.

"Jesus, I thank You for Your Word. I thank You for what You paid for on the cross. We call it into being now in Michal's body. We command all parasites and disease to leave her skin and organ systems and speak complete restoration to every cell in her body."

Again we saw no visible or instantaneous change. I left the baptism site for another meeting, continuing to thank God for what He was doing even though we could not see it yet. Faith is the evidence of things *not* seen. I knew we had done what Jesus asked, and He was pleased. The rest was up to Him.

When I returned home later that evening, my first stop was to check on Michal. Her face was shining. The sores that had covered her body were virtually gone. The swelling had reduced, and the scarring had dissolved. It was like looking at a different girl! Full of energy and life, she literally bounced out of the door to join the rest of our family for worship.

Michal, too, had come home. No, she was not moving in to live with us, but she had found her home in His heart. In the middle of her pain and sickness, she encountered the One who is love, and He healed her.

Papa, would You come and baptize me again in Your love, wash away the past and make all things new?

Mascara and a Machete

I never thought I could add land surveyor to my résumé, but in Sudan anything is possible. After God blessed us with our land we decided it would be a really good thing to find out with some accuracy how big it was and see if our proposed development plan would work. Having the correct measurements laid out before we began to build was somewhat important so that we did not put our first children's house in, say, the area for the administration office block. After three tries at hiring contracted workers to measure our land, three very different figures stared at us from their reports. We finally set out a-bushwhacking ourselves to measure it.

Tito, Eudita, Peter (our driver) and yours truly set off with a *panga* (machete), some paint, a hammer and, of course, the measuring tool of choice, a fifty-meter tape measure. It was a bonding time—one of those postcard moments that leave an indelible impression on your memory because of their absurdity. *A tape measure?*

There I was wearing a party skirt in the middle of the bush measuring our perimeter with a tape measure. The thought of it still makes me laugh. We giggled and sang, danced and prayed around the barely fenced periphery. It was a trek into the realm of the peculiar. Forty acres and many laughs later the mission was accomplished.

As I walked around our land with our Sudanese family, I really felt as though it was a homecoming in many ways. It was a beautiful day where the blue sky was rivaled only by the green bush and red dirt. Mango trees and coconut trees dotted the horizon. Birds chirped, and butterflies danced across our path. A random set of mud huts turned the scene into something out of adventure travelogues.

I had come home in more ways than one. I no longer felt the need to fit into someone else's box of missions or ministry. I was beginning to live loved by Papa. I was encountering a freedom to be myself even in the middle of the bush, all the while loving and honoring the people around me. If I wanted to look nice and dress up to go bushwhacking, I could. If I wanted to wear mascara, I could. I might live in the bush, but I did not have to look like it. God's Spirit offered freedom, and that freedom came from having a heart that had found its home in the Father's love. Everything else was just peripheral.

Religion is adept at building boxes and selling them as prime real-estate commodities for our hearts. Expectations create icons in which we live in a constant dance of conformity. What reputation am I measuring up to? Comparison is a compromise that can put us at risk of becoming an echo of someone else's song and losing the voice God gave us.

I am most fully effective when I am who God created me to be. I was not created to live in a box but to live in Papa's house. His house is where I am invited to become fully who He is calling me to be. He does not have cookie-cutter children.

It may seem silly, but standing waist deep in the bush in a party skirt wielding a panga felt like freedom. It was a little picture of the truth that when we do find our home in Jesus' heart, every part of us can be fully alive at the same time. God used mascara and a machete to call me deeper into living a life unboxed, free to respond to His love as I fully find my home in Him.

Visited by Jesus

Our older boys amaze me. They each have stories that are worthy of feature-length films. Seventeen, eighteen and nineteen years old, these boys have lived a journey that would make Hollywood take notice. But until now their stories have remained hidden threads in the fabric of a nation recovering from decades of war.

LOVE HAS A FACE

Their memories are reminders that the war was not so long ago. It was not so far away. And it was real.

Three of our boys came to live with us from a mountainous, isolated, landlocked region that borders southern Darfur. The people there were heavily affected by the war and experienced dynamics similar to those now happening in the neighboring region of Darfur. But for the most part, the pain of the peoples there was largely unseen by the outside world.

The childhoods and homes of these young men were decimated by war. As young as eight, nine and ten years old, they would run into the caves with the women when the armies came and hide there for weeks at a time, braving the darkness amid poisonous snakes and deep crevasses with no light and little to no food. All the while bombs surrounded them, and they feared they might never see their loved ones again.

Yet the faith of these boys is inspiring:

Mama, God did not forget us. He took care of us. The *antinofs* would come. You could hear them coming a long way off. They would drop bombs that would explode, and then people would get sick. Our skin would begin to burn. But God protected us. No one died. The northern armies would poison our wells. We had no other source of water. So we just prayed and drank the water anyway. And no one even got sick; it just cleaned out our intestines.

Their stories unfolded night after night as we sat around drinking our *cau-cau* (local coffee) by the fire. Their "man council," as they dubbed it, became a time for recalling God's faithfulness and probing into the deep issues of life around them. It was a time for daring to see. Home has become a favorite topic. You can understand why. Can you imagine what it means to find home when your world is at war? If ever I need a reminder of God's promise to make His home with us, I have to look no farther than these boys' stories of faith and God's faithfulness.

One Sunday morning I awoke to hear that one of these boys had had a dream the night before. Following are his own words describing that dream:

> So, it was last night when I had a good dream that we were visited by Jesus. Really it was just by the gate. We were sitting with these children here, and Jesus came, and everybody was scared. He told us not to be scared because He is our brother who always stays with us every day here at the compound. He has just come to visit us. He is sent by our heavenly Father to bring for us His greetings.

I told you greetings are important in Sudanese culture. Even God brings them when He visits here. He understands where we live.

Not only does Jesus want us to find our home in Him, but He also desires to make His home with us. How do I know this? He walked onto our compound and visited one of our boys to tell him so. He wants us to be at home in His presence and from there become the face of His love to a homeless world.

True worshipers worship in spirit and truth

8 Inside-out Kingdom

A small voice singing a simple chorus to Jesus is floating through my window. I do not even have to look to see which one of my precious five-year-olds it is. I would recognize Katia's (not her real name) clear, bell-like child's voice anywhere.

"*Ni we we tu bwarna, ni we we tu.*" ("It is only You, Jesus, it is only You.") She is sitting just under my window pouring her heart out to Him. My heart melts when I hear her sing.

Katia has been through so much already. She came to us shortly after we opened in December 2006. She is one of Benia's older sisters. (Remember the four-month-old infant who cost us three weeks of sleep back in chapter 2?) Katia is a quiet, shy little girl who easily could become lost amidst the drama surrounding her younger sisters and the work ethic of her overly responsible and utterly capable older sister, who at age six is taking charge of her siblings in her mother's absence.

But Katia is not forgotten. Of all our younger children she is one of the hungriest to learn of God's heart. She has memorized every worship song and can be heard singing them all around the compound. A delicate songbird from heaven, Katia does not need a lot of company to be happy. Her eyes often have a mystical look as if they are peering into another realm.

One night just after prayers Katia came to my door. She had something she wanted to show me. I bent down and took her in my arms. I about fell off my seat when she began to recite Genesis 1:1–2 in flawless English, with a huge grin of satisfaction on her face. She giggled at my shocked expression and proceeded to repeat the verses to make sure I got them. Then she sang me every worship song her heart could recall, cuddled into my arms and began to fall asleep.

Only months before, Katia's world was shattered. Her mother had hanged herself after being tormented by demons, and Katia was taken out of the only family she knew and deposited in our newly started center. Now here she was, sitting on my lap knowing she was loved and having conquered her first memory verse in a foreign language at the age of five. I was amazed that she wanted to recite the Bible, but what undid my heart was to see the look of joy and freedom in her eyes.

Katia's song is the sound of an inside-out Kingdom where the broken and the orphaned find who they truly are reflected in Love's eyes. It is the sound of an upside-down reality where the ash heaps of nations become the places chosen for the realm of heaven to emerge in power. Just like Katia sings, it really is "only You, Jesus."

Journey to Juba

In 2005, before Africa was fully on my radar screen, I was on a plane flying back to Colorado following a conference in Canada. I was seated at the bulkhead of the plane when I was overwhelmed with the awareness of God's presence.

It was as if Jesus had walked onto the plane and sat next to me. I saw Him step onto the plane wearing a T-shirt and jeans. He walked over and smiled at me as He sat down in the unoccupied seat to my left. I looked into the same eyes of love that had captured my heart as a little girl and just about melted.

About thirty minutes into the two-hour flight I was enjoying His presence when suddenly the roof of the plane appeared to vanish above me in a spiraling whirlwind. Now, being on an airplane and watching the roof above you disappear is slightly unnerving. I looked around me and rapidly ascertained that no one else was alarmed. *It must be one of those God things peculiar to me!* I thought.

I then was whisked into an encounter where Jesus and I danced on the crystal sea. I was no longer wearing my jeans and sweater but was clothed in a lovely, white ball gown, and Jesus was wearing His royal robes, every inch the King of kings. He walked up to me and asked, "May I have this dance?"

Instantly I was caught up in a whirling waltz where the scenery around me spun by out of the corner of my eye. It spun faster and faster until it was transformed and we were dancing in the slums and leper colonies of South Asia, then the garbage dumps of Africa, in refugee camps and red light districts. Jesus and I were dancing wherever lives had been broken and tossed aside.

And in each place we danced, the river of life flowed and the landscape was transformed.

The place that stands out the most in my memory of that encounter is the garbage dump. As Jesus and I danced in that dump, a river sprang up from beneath the mounds of rubbish and began to wash the land clean. As it touched the people, their bloated bellies became flat and their sores disappeared. I will never forget those images.

Recently I had to go to Juba on business. Juba is the seat of governmental affairs for southern Sudan, about a seven-hour drive north of Yei. On our return trip home, our route required us to drive through the Juba dump.

Five miles outside of the city center overflowing mounds of decaying garbage lined the road. Flies swarmed so thickly that if you opened your mouth you were likely to have two or three visitors. The dump lined the road for almost two and a half miles. Periodically we saw pockets of children and families scavenging for scraps to eat.

As we entered the dump I realized I had seen this place before. This was one of the trash heaps upon which Jesus and I had danced in my vision years before! I was so shocked I was not sure what to do with the revelation. His tangible presence began to fill our Land Rover. John, one of the pastors traveling with us, leaned over the seat and tapped my shoulder.

"Mama, should we stop and preach?"

"Yes! Peter, stop the car!"

Peter, our driver, brought the car to a halt, and John and I leapt out onto a pile of rotting refuse. The crowd of forty to fifty people raiding the latest dump deliveries looked up from their scavenging to see what the commotion was all about as the little white woman with one leg began to shout, "Good news! We are here to bring you a message of good news!"

Their curiosity got the better of them, and they put down their trash to come over and watch this spectacle in the dump. Soon John and I were surrounded by a crowd in black rags with sores on their skin. As I held the children who were eating maggot-laden food and told them of God's love for them amidst the swarms of flies, His love washed over us all. Heaven descended into that dump. Every person there prayed to receive Jesus. Not one turned Him down. Not one. And they asked us to come back. Blessed are the poor in spirit, the ones who know their need, for theirs is the Kingdom.

On our way home we prayed and listened to God's heart for the people we had just met. Peter looked at me and said with a smile, "Mama, a big church is going to start on the dump, and it will change Juba." John reminded me in the excited chatter that filled our journey home that Jesus was born not in a palace but in a dirty place like a dump. So we should look for such places. Our children wanted to go back to the dump with us to help us find more children who needed help and to join us in praying for the sick. Our family was catching God's heart for their own nation in increasing measure.

In response to the posturing, power plays and programs of the structured religious world that is alive and well here, Jesus gave us a big gift. He gave us an opportunity to go low, to go to the least. His Kingdom is an inside-out reality where as we lose we actually gain, and as we die we live. Jesus showed up because there in the middle of flies and filth He was welcome and wanted. To me that dump was the most beautiful location I had seen yet, because everyone wanted Him there.

It was an unexpected place of promise, and from there rivers of life will flow into a spiritually dry land. In God's upside-down, inside-out Kingdom, the trash heaps of the world will become some of His greatest places of outpouring.

It is not a plan that transforms the places of brokenness around me. It is a dance of love where every day I choose to stay low and close to His heart. It is a dance whose steps I still am just learning.

Waters of Healing, Rivers of Life

I have had ample chances here to practice the art of going lower in love.

Do you recall our commitment to put in a well for the community associated with our land? The well finally was finished, and we were in the truck headed to the official well-opening ceremony. Knowing that this community had at least in part been cursing us, I prayed for an extra-special message to convey God's heart to them. As soon as we arrived and I stepped off the truck, a tribal elder came up to me.

"You deceiver. All women are deceivers." What a lovely greeting! Apparently he was angry because we were late and they were waiting for us. We had been told the wrong starting time. I apologized profusely for any inconvenience or misunderstanding and began a rather tense march with the tribal leaders through the bush to the new well.

Everything in me wanted to tell them a thing or two, but I knew about God's upside-down Kingdom. When we are cursed, we bless. When we are reviled, we love.

Jesus, help. Show me their hearts. Show me what love looks like. Show me how to see Your Kingdom come here in power today.

As I walked with them God told me that this particular village had been cheated in the past. Promises that had been made to them had been broken repeatedly. They had been deceived and hurt, and they had held on to the pain in their hearts by refusing to forgive the ones who had hurt them.

We stood at the well, and they invited me to speak. I told them what God had shown me about their past and what they had suffered.

"Is this true? Have I spoken accurately?" I asked. Their faces revealed shock and disbelief that God would allow someone to see their pain.

I went on to tell them about living water. I told them that it was not an organization or humanitarian aid that brought this well to them. It was God's love.

"Every time you drink this clean water and your children drink this water, remember that God's love gave you a gift. He has given you a well in the natural to remind you that He Himself wants to give you living water for your spirits—water that will never run dry. If you drink this water you will be thirsty again. But if you drink the living water Jesus wants to give you, you will never thirst again."

As soon as the elders drank the water, something shifted. The mood changed from condemnation to celebration. Even the man who had been sure I was out to cast great deception on their lot began to smile. Soon, in place of cursing us, they began to bless us and thank God. Thirty seconds after the first drops of water from the well hit the ground a gentle rain began to fall. It was as if this blessed rain from heaven was sent to wash away the barrenness and curses from the land.

This moment was history in the making. In all of their remembrance these people had never seen a practical display of love like this. Sure, this village had heard a lot of talk, but God's Kingdom is not a matter of talk. It is a tangible, real demonstration of power.

The rain soon became a downpour that forced our team to take shelter in a local denominational church. While they bear the name "Christian," many of the religious structures here can be almost hostile to the Good News of knowing Jesus personally. This, however, was not the case that day!

Dancing and singing and celebration broke out, and no one wanted to leave. We prayed for the sick, and for the first time in that area the people saw God heal.

I have been on a quest for learning what it means to live in love and see God's Kingdom come on earth as it is in heaven. There in front of my eyes that day was a demonstration of the power of humility and love in action. Truly God's upside-down Kingdom rarely comes as we expect.

Unyielding Love

In the early morning light I was in my room preparing to walk yet again to our local hospital to check on our youngest infant, who was fighting for her life. She had come to us just three days earlier.

Images from the last 72 hours raced through my mind. She had arrived on our doorstep a mere eleven days old with an entourage of family members requesting help for the little bundle in their arms. Her grandmother agreed to move in and help us with her care. Her mother was an all-too-familiar statistic. She was one of eight women who die in childbirth here each day.

As they laid her in my lap, I looked down at the sleeping treasure. "What is her name?" I asked. *Akish*, they told me, which means "orphan." I quickly asked if the family would allow us to change her name. We could not call her "Orphan" because she was being adopted into a family, and it would not be a true name anymore. They readily agreed.

Later that day I went online to scour for the right name for this little life. *Papa, what do You call her?* After about an hour of prayer and searching in a dusty, hot Internet shack, I found it. With the family's permission we changed this baby's name to *Azeezah Adanna*, meaning "cherished one of her Father."

On Azeezah's first night with us we discovered that her whole body was wracked with infection. She began to gasp for breath, and a death rattle filled her lungs. To her grandmother's dismay she cried all night long in great pain. The next morning we took her immediately to the hospital and had been with her night and day since. But the medical capabilities here are extremely limited. We had been doing all we could do, rotating shifts and spending long hours holding her, praying for her and speaking life into her.

Two days into this saga the nurses had tried to assure me she was doing better because she had stopped crying and was sleeping. But I knew in my spirit that she had slipped into a coma. Late the second night I had returned home to get a few hours of sleep.

About four o'clock that morning I had been awakened with a vision of Jesus sweeping up our newest little baby into His arms and taking her home to His Father's house. Every cell in my being wanted to interpret that vision figuratively. How could I fall so much in love with a little messenger of His grace in less than three days? Such love had to be born of heaven. It certainly was not natural.

As I dressed to head back to the hospital I heard a knock at my door. My heart sank. I knew. When I opened the door I was not surprised to see our family crowded in the doorway to tell me the news. Azeezah had been taken home to heaven about four in the morning.

I got my things together and walked not to the hospital but to the mud hut village behind our rental compound to meet and sit with the family as they grieved. They ushered me into a dim mud tukal. I knelt at the bed where Azeezah's little body lay.

I asked Jesus if He wanted me to pray for her to come back to life. I immediately saw her smiling in His arms. He said, *No. Is it okay if she grows up here in her Father's house?* Tears rolled down my face and soaked her small frame. As much as we all had believed for healing so that she could grow up in our home, I knew that she was very much alive in her Papa's house. I wept, holding her small body in my embrace, grieving yet knowing that while her body was there, little Azeezah was not.

I reached out and held her grandmother, an elderly Shillok woman from a northern part of South Sudan bearing the tattoos of her tribe. I wept as she wept. I was learning a little more about what it is like to be Sudanese. A little more about living in a place of utter helplessness. A little more about being sacrificial love in the place of pain. This, too, is the Gospel. This, too, is His inside-out Kingdom. It is not only raising the dead; it is also weeping with those who weep.

Then all around me, I saw another kind of miracle taking place. As I knelt holding her, a community began to open its arms to us. I was not trying to be a good missionary or spiritually identify with these people. I literally felt as if my heart were breaking. Yet as they saw my brokenness, the community of Shillok and Kawkwa ladies came around to comfort me. The whole family would not stop saying thank you.

I knelt in the dirt holding Grandma as tears streamed down both our faces and turned the ground around us into mud. Later we watched together as they lowered Azeezah's sheet-wrapped body into the grave and packed dirt on top of it.

The grave looked final. It was not. It was an illusion. Through my tears I could see angels joining the community, and I again saw Jesus holding Azeezah as she smiled and giggled, no longer the pain-racked, malnourished little one who had come to our doorstep a few days ago.

Some might read this account of Azeezah's short life and think, *What a waste.* But not one second of her little life was wasted. Azeezah became a prophetic message of God's heart to us. She arrived with the name *Akish*—"orphan." We renamed her *Azeezah Adanna*, "cherished daughter of her Father." And her Father had indeed taken her home to live in His house in heaven.

In Sudan a generation who once were called orphans are now called cherished sons and daughters of their Father. These precious children are learning to live from heaven to earth, knowing their place in their Father's house. And from that reality, villages and communities are opening their hearts to His love. This is the Kingdom.

Death did not win. It never does in Jesus. Azeezah's message lives on. And we still choose to believe that God's love is stronger than death and more unyielding than the grave.

Army of Love

Azeezah's legacy continued to change lives. We found out months later what a great impact her story was having.

We live in a recovering war zone. When I first arrived it was not uncommon to hear gunfire at night. We were surrounded by soldiers from the Sudanese People's Liberation Army (SPLA), and many of them still had automatic weapons from the war years. One day on the roundabout near our rental property, some men decided to brandish their weapons in my direction. It seemed to be a macho thing more than anything else, but who can tell with a loaded AK-47 pointed in your direction? I think they just wanted to see my reaction, and I am certain the reaction they saw that day was quite unexpected. I knew I had a choice. I could choose fear, or I could choose the love that disarms it. I managed to use my intentional ignorance of such matters as machine guns to my full advantage. I also chose to take quite literally the verse that says perfect love drives out all fear.

"Wow, way cool! Say, what kind of gun is that?" I asked them with a huge smile on my face. "Is that like an AK-47 or a Kalashnikov? I can never tell." My heart was beating a bit faster than normal, but they did not need to know that.

They were so flustered by my visible lack of fear that they put down their weapons. Sensing an opportune moment, I decided to push the envelope just a bit farther.

"So has that gun ever raised the dead?"

Puzzled expressions with a pregnant pause. "Uh, no."

"Hmmm, so your guns only kill people, right?"

They looked at me as if I were crazy. "Yes."

"Well, if your guns can only kill people and God's love can raise the dead, maybe His love is a more powerful weapon than your gun."

Silence.

"So if you really want to win what you are fighting for, perhaps you should look into fighting with weapons of His love!"

Not long after this encounter a local leader from the SPLA visited our compound. We shared many things over a bowl of beans, including my little weapons analogy. He looked at me in all seriousness and invited us to do a seminar in the barracks on what it means to be an army of love. Suddenly one of the most unlikely candidates in history was going to teach tactical military training on love to 120 soldiers!

When the appointed day arrived the road was practically washed out, so we almost did not make the sixty-mile journey. But angels stirred Lemonade onward, and we crossed the great, muddy divide. Our challenges increased when the driver-side windshield wiper went out yet again, and we had to stop every few hundred yards to sling a sopping towel out the window at the windshield. Seeing where you are driving does help. After three hours bouncing in the car and manually wiping the windows, we pulled up tired, wet and an hour late.

A waiting entourage of soldiers greeted me. They were praying the rain would stop because we were meeting under a bamboo frame loosely covered by barely-there tarps, and too much water on those tarps could cause our group to become subject to a waterfall. I stepped under the makeshift accommodations and greeted the group in Juba Arabic. Their serious faces burst into grins and their applause sounded louder than the rain around us.

I began to preach my heart out on what it means to be the face of love. I told them about the power of God's love that never fails. I told them that our weapons and strategies fail, but His love never does. This message then led unexpectedly into a powerful ministry time.

"Who wants more love?" I asked. "Who wants to live a life of love fully expressed?" Every hand went up, and half the room came forward to join me kneeling in the dirt and mud. At the end they asked if we would please come back.

Before we finished we opened up the floor to comments, which is a cultural tradition here in this tribal society. When you are finished preaching, everyone gets to commentate on your message.

One small-framed man got up and began to speak with a fiery passion. I listened to him and slowly recognized him as baby Azeezah's father. His testimony nearly rendered me speechless.

"The first day I brought my daughter to these people I had heard of, they welcomed her and took her in their arms. They hugged her and kissed her. Often we do not even show such affection to our own children. And here these people come from so far away. They give up everything to come and suffer with us and show such love to a people who are not their own."

He went on to recount in detail our many hours of sitting in the hospital. He recalled my crying with them in the dirt at the funeral. He charged the gathering: "I have never seen love like this anywhere from anyone before. These people do not preach anything other than what they live. Listen to them."

Tears began to flow down my cheeks. Months after Azeezah's earthly life had ended, God's Kingdom was still breaking through because of simple acts of love. This father who had lost everything looked into my eyes with all the intensity of heaven and spoke nothing less than a commission: "Please take this message of love all over Sudan. It is what our people need. It is the only thing that will save this nation."

Indeed it is a message that is needed not only in Sudan but also throughout the world. God's love is the only thing that never fails and will meet the needs of our day.

The Unexpected, the Unpredictable and the Unlikely

Here in the bush of Sudan, God's upside-down Kingdom is evident. Here in one of the most forgotten areas of the world,

One of our fearsome pray-ers

God uses the unlikeliest people to bring about His unpredictable plans and His unexpected miracles. A tiny one-legged white woman from across the world, a bunch of at-risk children who have already lived more in their little lives than most adults, a bunch of simple village mamas and soldiers wielding AK-47s—our Father somehow uses all of us to weave together secret treasures and riches hidden in darkness.

Here in Sudan my life is becoming a treasure hunt to find royalty by the roadside and diamonds in the dust. Every day here my vision is challenged. Can I see past the corruption and the defilement to find the treasure worth extracting? Do I have Kingdom eyes to see how King Jesus longs to come and make His beauty known? If I am to become His message, then I must see His way. Every day my prayer remains: *Jesus, let me love with Your love and see with Your eyes.*

"How many nations do I want to bring to King Jesus?" I ask myself. When I asked the same question to our little family gathering, their cry reverberated throughout all eternity and caused darkness even a world away to shake as they shouted, "All of them!"

Could this be the beginning of a movement? After all, Jesus changed the world with twelve very unlikely candidates. It makes me breathe a sigh of relief. That puts our little fledgling group on pretty good footing. I happen to think the devil is very, very scared of my three-year-olds. They know how to pray so that heaven responds. I learn from them every day. Three-year-olds who are loved have almost no fear. They are dangerous to the kingdom of darkness.

"Jesus, make the sickness go away. Devil, go away in Jesus' name. Amen." I mean, what can the enemy say to that one? All heaven backs up their prayers!

My personal favorite prayer was offered by one of my little ones who crawled up onto my lap and prayed: "Jesus, please bring Mama [me] her leg. I know it is in heaven. Bring it here now. Leg, grow. Thank you." If I ever had a doubt of my leg being restored, my children's faith has sure helped to banish it!

I have been privileged to witness the blind see, the deaf hear and paralytics walk, but some of the greatest miracles I have seen have come through His love being poured out on broken hearts and lives. I regularly see glimpses of His unexpected comings: my children, once orphaned, now laying hands on the blind and watching their eyes come into focus; little lives who once lived on the streets now bringing a cup of cold water to a visitor and helping in the kitchen with dinner; those who had no schooling now studying and learning to dream bigger than the world around them.

Maybe the Kingdom is as simple as a well in a village, as simple as a little child who no longer has to drink from disease-ridden, stagnant cesspools. Maybe the Kingdom looks like clean, flowing water ready to drink—a visible expression tapped from the depths of God's heart. Wells of life opened, wells of salvation and healing released. Could revival simply be the face of love in action that becomes a voice of truth in the night?

Maybe revival looks different each time it comes. In Scripture, did Jesus ever heal the same way twice? It seems He liked to be unpredictable. His moving was a bit like the wind. Sometimes it was loud. Sometimes it was seen. Often it was quiet or hidden and recognized only after the fact for what it was. But it was always love. Love was His meaning. He had no other. I have had to watch my heart, for it is easy to box God in with *my* expectations of what His Kingdom should look like here.

Perhaps God desires a movement of love so supernatural that a nation is changed by those who dare to dance in doorways of death and call forth unstoppable life. I am no longer satisfied with attending or participating in a meeting called revival. I want to live a revival reality and carry His glory into the darkness. Our goal is nothing less than lives and communities transformed from the inside out and turned upside-down by love. That is revival.

I have not yet arrived. But I am on a daily journey through mud and dust, need and faith. Perhaps I am a little farther down the road with each day that comes and goes, but I really do ñot want to take my eyes off Him to assess my own progress.

He has become my goal. His Kingdom comes as I live from the inside out every day. I cannot give away what I do not have. My inner reality has to be hidden in who He is in order for me to see the reality of who He is change the world around me.

I am learning that the Kingdom is love. It is joy. It is peace. It is life lived in the power of the Holy Spirit. It cannot be lived any other way. But love is the foundation, the focus, the how, the why, the reason, the promise, the call, the catalyst, the mandate, the mantle, the answer, our all in all—because love is who He is.

And this I know. Love never fails.

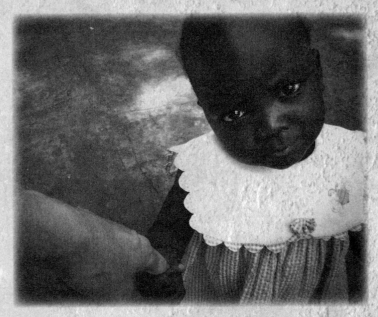

"Mama, tali . . ." (Mama, come)

9 Just Breathe

I have shared with you that our life has a bit of a slower pace here in Africa. It is true. They call it African time. Our culture is relational. I learned rapidly that the people in front of me had to take priority over the projects around me. There is something beautiful about that. It is reminiscent of the Kingdom. But it is also unnerving at times. Some days I have wondered how anything manages to get accomplished. And some days it does not. Everything happens with its own unique Sudanese rhythm.

With many children, local staff, missionaries and visitors, several churches and even more projects, it would be easy to feel stressed. Sometimes I do. Jesus clearly expressed His wonderful sense of humor when He sent me to Sudan. I can just imagine Him discussing it with the Father: "Let's send a super-achieving, Type A personality to the bush to help her learn she cannot do it and she needs to chill." He reminds me daily that the only measure of success in His eyes is living loved each day and loving one life at a time.

As a child with lots of medical procedures, I learned that holding my breath was a way to control my world. It was a way to anticipate and maybe stave off impending pain. But I could only hold my breath for so long! On those days here in Sudan when all chaos breaks loose and I am tempted to sheer frustration, Papa says to me, *Honey, just breathe.* It is His way of telling me that He really does have everything—even the seeming chaos and crises—under His control. And if He is in control, then I do not need to be. All I need to do is trust Him. All I need to do is be with Him. All I need to do is breathe.

Just breathe.

One day as I was eating a newly ripened mango the children had ruthlessly disengaged from the branch of our compound tree, Jesus turned my afternoon snack into a message: *Rest is when the work becomes as simple as bearing fruit. Fruit cannot be forced. Mangoes grow only in mango season, and if it is not mango season then enjoy papayas instead. That is rest.*

Here surrounded by mud cathedrals and mango trees I am learning more what it means just to be, to breathe, to rest and to love.

Heaven Has a Candy Aisle

One afternoon I was talking with the children about how we were planning to have fun together in the coming days. One of our older boys who was helping me translate paused and with a puzzled look on his face asked, "Mama, what is *fun?*"

Now how was I to explain the concept of fun to a culture that does not even have a word for it?

"Well, sweetheart, *fun* is when you are doing something you like; you are having a good time and something is enjoyable. That's what you call *fun.*"

"Oh, Mama, I see. Thank you very much. Let God bless you."

We could have talked more about fun and provided more dictionary definitions, but I am a firm believer in experiential learning. One of our short-term volunteers was about to celebrate her 21st birthday while she was staying with us. What better excuse to put fun into practice than to throw a party!

I am convinced God loves parties. After all, He has prepared for us the greatest party of all time—a wedding feast—when we get to heaven, right? So when in doubt, throw a party!

Well, here in our fine bush resort in the southern reaches of the Sudanese outback, party planning is not the easiest. Planning an impromptu birthday bash in the bush is not as simple as stopping off at Macy's for party favors. Here in the middle of this muddy metropolis there is no Dillard's or local branch of Nordstrom. No, not even a Walgreens. Nope. Our only option is a small corner shop in a dusty border town in northern Uganda.

On our regular trip to Arua just before the eve of the awaited celebration, we had the foresight to pick up 96 heart-shaped lollipops. We also were hugely blessed to pick up some packages at the post office there. One of them contained some DVDs.

The evening plans expanded to include a special debut showing of our newly arrived copy of VeggieTales' *Dave and the
Giant Pickle.*

Evening was approaching, and we began to set up the generator, speakers and projector. It was amazing how word traveled
with no advertisement! Our bamboo fence was, shall we say,
breathable. If you really wanted to come onto our compound
you just pushed a few bamboo pieces aside and came in. The
neighborhood children were adept at that trick. Before we knew
it word had gotten out that there was a video on the Iris Compound, and our crowd began to grow.

We had intended for this event to be a small family celebration
of ninety or so. We had 96 lollipops, enough for our kids and
staff family. But by the time we were ready to pass them out,
our crowd was easily more than double that number.

What were we going to do? Did we show the video and forego
the candy until later? If we ran out, our celebration would turn
into an imminent riot. Stories of water turning into wine at
a party long ago and a small boy's lunch feeding thousands
paraded through my memory. Images of small sock-covered
hands with steaming cups of hot cocoa from a few years earlier in Texas came to my mind. *Jesus, are You telling me what
I think You are?*

We eyed the growing crowd of children cramming onto the
rickety wooden benches set in our front yard. It was now or
never. We prayed over the heart-shaped sweets and thanked Papa
for what we knew had to be a miracle to come.

One of our visitors was not sure about how the multiplication
anointing applied to candy. When we asked him to help pass out

the lollipops, he looked at the candy then looked at the crowd. He weighed the situation, and the precarious place of extreme faith where we were teetering dawned on him.

"Uhumm, do you, uh, have a plan . . . B?" he asked.

"No plan B. You start at the back, okay?"

And guess what?

We had enough candy for every child and every adult on the compound to have a special birthday sweet. We even had one sucker left over! God has a candy factory for moments such as these.

I was elated! Who would not be? It was not exactly the feeding of the five thousand, but it was awesome to see 96 sweets feed over two hundred people.

The celebration was a raving success. The VeggieTales DVD made our entire compound laugh, cheer, ooh and aah. They were not quite sure what to do with singing vegetables that had personality. Were vegetables supposed to dance? Yet the theme song from that movie could not have been more appropriate. Intrepid Dave, played by Junior Asparagus, took on the feared Giant Dill Pickle, Goliath, as he sang:

> You're big, I'm little.
> My head comes only to your middle,
> But with God little guys can do big things, too.

That night our children went to sleep with their hearts echoing songs of victory over defeated giants and the taste of heaven's provision in their mouths. God does indeed like parties, and heaven did indeed have a candy aisle.

The evening reminded me that in this Kingdom I am called to look with new eyes. I am called to a supernatural life of passing out lollipops when it seems there are not enough, dancing in the storms around me and giving parties for people who have never had them before. All of this comes as I learn more each day simply to breathe and be in the One who is love.

Raising the Bar

The unpaved road of following God's heart has led me to many places. They all have had one major thing in common: They all have required me to breathe. Parties in the bush, mission trips to other African nations, object lessons from everyday happenings—all have revolved around this theme of taking a deep breath.

I recently was invited to travel to Ghana for the first time. Yes, I know, this is a book about Sudan, not Ghana, but God used this journey to teach me more about relaxing and trusting Him and, yes, breathing more deeply. Remembering what God taught me in Ghana has helped me greatly here on Sudanese soil.

My first full day in Ghana I went with a small evangelism team through the crowded, twisting alleys of a Ghanaian slum. I stepped into the tin-roofed menagerie and instantly felt at home. You see, slums are my absolute favorite places to be. Yes, it is nice when that rare mission trip takes you to a hotel that is nicer than your usual living accommodations, and any place with running water tops my normal housing. But if our team drops me off in the slums for the week I am a happy woman.

The day was teeming with rain. But for us that was part of heaven's plan. The downpour forced our little group to take shelter in a small restaurant of sorts, and amidst the seeming setbacks and potential agitation my Papa reminded me, *Sweetheart, take a deep breath.*

The iron sheet roof leaked in at least three places, making small pools on the floor. The bamboo walls allowed the wind and the light to come in, along with a little rain. But it was mostly dry, comparably speaking. Crates of liquor lined one wall, and several bleary-eyed customers sat on chairs that barely looked like they would hold them.

Our group evened out the numbers, and we all sat there looking at one another. Two precious little girls peeked into the room from the doorway. I decided to try out my Twi greeting that I had painstakingly learned from our hotel guard that morning. When in a new land, love can look like learning to say hello and thank you all over again.

"*Ete sen?*" I asked. (These words actually sound like *wa-ho-ta-zen* and mean "How are you?")

"*Eye!*" (*Wa-ho-ye*—"Fine") came their surprised and enthusiastic reply.

The rather quiet crowd burst into smiling chatter in response to a little white woman trying out their language. Our translator took off explaining who we were and why we were there. Were there any people who would like prayer?

One by one they came forward. Pain left. Fevers were banished. Sickness disappeared. Drunken stupors vanished as the love of Jesus permeated the atmosphere. Everyone wanted to either receive Jesus for the first time or come back to Him after wandering away. And while all this was happening one of the little angels in the doorway curled up and fell fast asleep in my lap. Her older sister played with my strange hair. It would not stay braided like hers.

One tall woman with matted hair and wild eyes stands out in my memory of that day. She entered the restaurant intoxicated and wanting more drink for her pain. She was in the middle of arguing with someone behind a makeshift counter when the reality of what was happening with our little group gripped her. She came over asking for prayer and literally fell at our feet.

"I want to be free from alcohol!" she cried in a desperate voice.

"Do you know Jesus? He is the One who can set you free."

"No."

"Would you like to meet Him? He loves you very much."

"Yes."

Just that simply, heaven won for itself one more life for the Lamb's reward. We introduced her to the One who gave everything to set her free and give her life. Her wild eyes began to calm, and her tormentors loosened their grasp. She left without purchasing the drink she came for. She left with hope for a new life.

The small group that had gathered with us asked, "Can we have a church here?"

I replied almost without thinking, "You already do. We just had our first service."

One man could read and had a Bible. He had actually had some ministry education at one point but had fallen away from following Jesus. Our translator agreed to mentor him, and a

Outreach on the unpaved road

baby church was born. The rain relented, and we left for other West African adventures.

On our way out I mentioned to our interpreter, "Wow! There were a lot of people drinking early in the day in that restaurant."

An amused look crossed his face. "Michele, that was not a restaurant. That was a bar. You guys just planted a church in a bar."

Wowie zowie, God! That was easy! Sort of like breathing.

God's Kingdom comes even in Ghanaian slums and back-alley bars. Jesus liked to go to the rough-around-the-edges people and places in His day, too. He still does. And He is raising the bar in my life on what love looks like.

I am learning it is less about what I do or how much I accomplish. It is all about becoming the message I am called to bring.

Whether I am in Africa or America or anywhere in-between, fruit that remains grows out of a life intimately connected to Him. All I have to do is breathe. Just breathe.

It Is a Dance

I have gotten some things right on this journey. But I have gotten a lot of things wrong, too. One of those things is my "secret place" time with Jesus. It is not the big things that get in the way. It is the little things that distract and detract from time that should be spent with Him. I came to realize that on one of my trips to Uganda. It was easier to see what I was facing when I was not facing it so closely.

My little Ugandan guesthouse became a place of a momentary epiphany on that trip. The only witness to my revelation was a family of prehistoric-size cockroaches that scuttled into the dark corners of the room when I turned on the lights.

After a long soak in a tub I was not surprised to see my skin lighten about three shades. There went my so-called tan. I still had not managed the knack of the bucket bath. It was the first time in months that I had had any time truly alone. Remember that my home is a veritable fishbowl.

It was the first time I had slowed down long enough to realize that Jesus was watching my busy pace, my overflowing days and my crowded life. He was just watching me and waiting for me to notice that He was not as intent on my schedule as I was. I looked into His eyes and realized that I was getting the loving-others part right. I was seeing and stopping for the one in front of me. But I had forgotten that He was the most important One

I could ever stop for. His gaze held no condemnation. It held only invitation.

Suddenly I was taken into a vision where I was standing in a vast harvest field. It expanded as far as my eyes could see in every direction. It was lit with faint pre-dawn light. The sun was just beginning to touch the distant horizon.

The picture was so immense that I was overwhelmed. Where would I even begin to harvest that field? How would I start? I looked around me. I saw no tools, no bag, nothing at all to begin gathering this huge harvest.

In this vision Jesus walked up to me in the middle of that field. His face was shining. His eyes were smiling. He came so close to me that all I could see were His beautiful eyes. I could not look away, not even to see the harvest. He took me by the hand, and we began to dance. The field twirled by out of the corner of my eyes, but my gaze was locked with His and He alone was my focus.

"This is what I want," He said. "*This* is what I want. I want you to live a life with your eyes fixed on Me. As we dance together the harvest will come in. It is not about a plan; it is all about a dance."

Was I planning great exploits for Jesus? Or was I dancing with Him, letting Him fill all my vision and become my Everything?

I realized I had been lamenting my lack of resources and the huge task ahead of me. I was fixated on the field when Jesus wanted me to be focused on His face. He did not want me to settle and get by with romantic notions about Him. He wanted my heart, the core of who I am, to surrender to being romanced by Him, to be overtaken by His love. He wanted me to be so captivated by His gaze that He would become all I see.

His words resounded in my heart. It is not a plan that will win the world. It is a dance.

I do not have to be worried about success or failure, greatness or obscurity. All I have to do is find who I am in Love's eyes. All I have to do is be a little girl in the arms of her Papa, knowing she is loved not for anything she has done or achieved but simply because He loves her. I can stand on His feet and let Him lead, knowing that as we dance together the harvest will come in.

This, too, is rest.

Created for Another Realm

I travel a lot sharing what God has done and is doing in our midst. Recently I had the occasion of being blessed with a snorkeling trip on some of my travels.

As I mentioned, I am a Florida girl. I learned to swim before I learned to walk. I love snorkeling. I love the water. I love the fish. I love the utter peace and quiet that surrounds me when I stick my head just under the surface and all goes silent. I love the metaphorical significance of breathing in another realm and meeting God there. It has everything to do with life in the bush—even when oceans are thousands of miles away.

This, however, was no ordinary snorkeling tour! My first surprise came when our tour guide had us put on uniformly ugly, ill-fitting life vests inflated with hot air that served more to get in the way than anything else and then marched us out to the beach. He then began a lesson that could be entitled "Introduction to Your Mask 101." How hard is it to figure out a snorkeling mask? My friends and I just looked at one another. This was so bizarre it was almost comical. To add to the satire of the moment, it started to rain. We were made to stand in the rain while listening to the explanation of the proper use of the snorkel.

"The snorkel goes in your mouth. Keep the tip above the water line. Then breathe normally." No! I thought it went in my ear and was attached to my iPod.

Once we actually made it into the water, my second surprise came. Our tour guide was a thinly veiled aquatic drill instructor, commonly known in boot camp as the feared D.I. Couldn't we just enjoy snorkeling in this other realm for ourselves? Oh, no! We had to follow our snorkeling D.I., who insisted on us keeping in formation as he yelled at us to keep up the pace.

"You in the back!" (He was referring to me—I do not like being herded.) "Keep it up, keep it up, KEEP IT UP!"

Every two minutes our specially assigned tour guide would shout, "Are you okay? Everyone comfy? You in the back, I said *keep up!*" Then he would make us stop so he could announce, "There is an angel fish on your left and a coral formation on your right."

I had just entered the realm of extreme absurdity. I began to look not for unique fish but for the underwater camera guy filming for *Candid Camera*. He never did appear. But I did ask Jesus what He was saying in all this. It was too bizarre not to have some object lesson attached to the experience.

Breathing through my snorkel (which does not go in my ear—I am glad I found that out!) after being yelled at for the umpteenth time to keep up, I heard Jesus laughing. I began to chuckle myself. What was I going to do but laugh with such a scenario around me? Little did I realize the joke was on me.

Stroke after stroke, revelation dawned. Jesus was teaching me a powerful lesson: If I was not careful I could become the snorkel drill instructor! Ouch! He was showing me that if I did not stay submerged in the realm of God's presence myself, then I would be at risk of simply taking people on tours of the supernatural. If I were not careful I would be doing nothing more than focusing on safety, keeping the ones I led afloat with ill-fitting carbon-copy containers of hot air and protecting them from going too deep.

My mind filled with images of my children in Sudan all snorkeling in perfect formation with identical vests. Amusing? Maybe. Horrifying? Definitely. No one dared swim to the depths. The pressure to conform and stay on the surface was too strong. Then they began to compare their vests with one another. Hers is more inflated than mine. His is better looking. *Help me, Jesus!*

I did not want to herd my children or anyone else from meeting to meeting, checking every two minutes to see if they were comfortable or not. No! I wanted them to be free to explore for themselves the supernatural realm in which they were created to live and breathe without a tour guide or drill instructor. When it was all said and done, I did not want them to come ashore and say, "Wasn't that nice? We saw an angel fish, hallelujah!" I did not want them to leave with only an experience but no revelation.

A few days later I had the opportunity to snorkel again, this time without the tour guide. For three hours I floated in the aqua waters soaking in the understanding that all I have to do is float in His ocean of love and breathe. When I stay submerged in Him, I overflow from the realm in which I am immersed. Float in His love, then live in His flow.

That day I began to learn that His presence has a rhythm much like the rhythm of the ocean. Breathe in to the depths to drink Him in, and then breathe out to the shorelines of nations and circumstances to pour out His love on each person I meet. Breathe in to be with Him, then out to be with people. His is a holy rhythm of love like a heartbeat. As I soak and drink deeply of Him, I am saturated and have something to offer the ones around me.

I was not created for this realm. My children in Sudan were not created for this realm. Floating in the blue waters half a world away, I became increasingly convinced that we were created to live in the realm of our King and from there to manifest His Kingdom wherever we go. It really was that easy. Float in His love. Stay submerged in His heart. Breathe Him in and then watch His realm break through our lives everywhere we go. It was the supernatural life for which we were created where His natural becomes our normal.

Do you remember Gloria, the blind Ugandan woman whose eyes God healed? That miracle happened on my way home from my little snorkeling revelation experience. It was a miracle that happened not because I worked really hard but because I was learning to breathe and to rest. God was proving to me that floating in His ocean of love really did release the flow of His supernatural power.

I decided to take a stand. No more snorkel tours of the supernatural for me! I want to be so continuously filled with the love of God that I leak His love onto everyone I meet. I want to learn this rhythm of the deep. Float, flow, hide, give, love, drink, live and above all else do not forget to breathe.

The Ability to Respond

Recent years have brought some storms in my life. Yet how would I ever learn to dance—or breathe—in the midst of a storm without a storm? Jesus has used the stormy squalls often as compressed learning opportunities.

One storm occurred over a period of about six months in which I was constantly sick. A never-ending array of illnesses barraged my already battered immune system: malaria five times, parasites, unknown bacteria, staff infections and finally chronic fatigue syndrome. I was not being kind to myself. I pushed myself way too hard in the name of being a tough missionary and royally flunked my lessons on rest.

Soon I was so weak I could barely walk across the compound. I was getting progressively worse and lost four sizes in three weeks. I was in constant pain, severely fatigued and beyond desperate. The visiting doctor ordered me to bed rest, threatening to send me back to the United States from Sudan. I told her I was on my way to see a certain Specialist in Mozambique (yes, a Specialist with a capital S).

"What! There are no specialists in Mozambique."

"Mine is coming especially to meet me."

In June 2007 I arrived at Iris Ministries' center in Mozambique for a periodic staff retreat. Thin, frail and pasty, I had a greenish glow that concerned many of my friends. There was talk about possible hospital visits. But I did not travel thousands of miles to visit hospitals that were not much better than the ones in Uganda. I had a word from heaven, and I was holding on to it for dear life. Dr. Jesus was going to heal me.

I joined the caravan of staff converging on a hotel in Bilene to reconnect and worship together for the weekend. The first day I was so sick I could barely contemplate eating the beautiful food to which we were being treated. When would Jesus come and heal me? That night I lay on my face in worship because I was weak and the room was spinning.

The next morning came and went uneventfully. The second afternoon included a testimony time. One precious family working in northwest Mozambique shared and sang a song their daughters had written in the field. As they sang I felt waves of God's presence wash over me. I slid off my seat to the floor. Soon God's presence weighed so heavily upon me that I could not move—for seven hours.

I lay there literally magnetized to the floor. I did not see anything. I did not hear anything. I was fully cognizant but unable to get up. Break time and dinner came and went. Still I could not move. The evening worship came and went. People danced joyfully all around me. Still there I was. Someone graciously turned me over halfway through the evening.

The evening session finished, and people trailed to their rooms. I felt the weight begin to lift and slowly regained mobility. I did not feel anything notable during that time. I saw no visions. I heard no great audible revelations. But I got up healed!

The next day I ran, walked and danced at every opportunity. In receiving this healing I had done nothing but breathe. Perhaps that was His point.

In the following days, Jesus began to speak to me that He did not create me to be responsible but to be response-able. In other words, He wanted me to be able to respond to Him in relationship.

I asked Jesus what I needed to do. *What should I do, Lord, in the face of what looks and feels some days like standing nose to nose with a thousand-foot-high tidal wave of darkness? What should I do in the face of overwhelming need and a dwindling bank account?*

His reply: *Let go.*

Let go of what, Lord?

Let go of the need to be responsible.

What a shocker. Ever since my cognitive understanding began to form, everything in my world told me I had to be responsible. Good people were responsible people. It was how I was raised. It was how I looked at myself. It was how I looked at ministry. Furthermore, I knew that the world looked at our ministry in Sudan and said, "Look at all those children! Wow, you are responsible for so much!" The Church saw the promises Jesus gave us and said, "Wow, what a lot of responsibility Jesus has given you!" Somehow I had begun to believe that myth called responsibility, and it turned what had been spontaneity into suffocation in my soul. It made even breathing hard work. The storm around me stopped being an opportunity to dance with Jesus and started to look like a sentence of drowning.

All the while, Jesus was saying, *No!*

Slowly I began to realize that Jesus did not give me His promises for Sudan as a responsibility to carry. He gave me His promises as a playground to embrace with Him. All He desired was my ability to respond to Him. That lie of false responsibility actually stole the joy and even the ability to respond to the spontaneous moving of His Spirit.

I was created to live in a love relationship with Papa, Jesus and the Holy Spirit that was based on *response-ability*. I was called to live in a place that enabled me to respond to His promptings. You might call it trust. I am not responsible for what He calls me into; I am simply to be response-able in the midst of His call.

It is much easier than I ever thought! Freedom really is that free. It felt a little like flying—or maybe floating in the ocean without a snorkel drill instructor.

Rest. Respond. Love. Let go. Let God. Breathe.

The Kingdom belongs to such as these

10 The Edge of the Map

A thin, solemn-faced woman came to our compound this week. She was carrying a small bundle. Her infant daughter had the face of an old woman. Her little malnourished body was not much more than bones, and she cried weak cries from sunken cheeks. Her eyes were flat and dull. She was the embodiment of her name: *Suffering*.

So many children here are named after the harsh realities of life: suffering, anger, unwanted, sadness, orphan. Their names are descriptive of the circumstances surrounding their earliest hours and days.

I looked into Suffering's two-month-old eyes that were just beginning to focus on the world around her. I picked up her frail frame and held her eye to eye with me. I just could not call her Suffering. She did not bring suffering into the heart of the Father. She brought joy.

"*Ita ma* Suffering. *Ita Faraha.*" ("You are not Suffering. You are Joy.")

I heard this mother's familiar story. After she gave birth she had no milk for her baby. Her daughter's first two months in this world were spent on a diet of cornmeal and water. This child was a fighter. Many babies would not have survived this long. The mother was from a tribal homeland far away. Her husband had been taken away to fight on some distant front line, and she had no one to help her—no one to show her love. This baby had indeed been born into a world of suffering. But Jesus does not define us by our circumstances.

I look forward to watching Faraha (Joy) grow and begin to thrive. I look forward to getting to know her mother and seeing God's love reach deep into another family to bring healing from the inside out.

Little Faraha got me thinking. The world often tries to define us by the facts of our surroundings. For me it is the fact that I have one leg and use crutches. For others the facts might be growing up on the wrong side of town or making mistakes they later regretted. But Jesus does not define us by our past or our present.

We are not "Suffering" to Him. We are not "The Girl with One Leg" or "The Poor Kid" or "The Druggie." Neither are we "The Rich Boy" or "The Party Girl." He does not define any of us by labels.

He calls us by name. He sees where we are, but He does not equate that with our identity. And when the world calls us something we are not in His eyes, He has no problem with the redemption of a name change.

Faraha reminded me of that this week. Love sees beyond where a person is to who that person is. Faraha was not destined to a life of suffering. She was created to be the Joy of her Papa in heaven and to bring joy to the world around her.

Until They All Have Names

Jesus has been speaking to me more about how revival has a name. I see each person God brings me as a potential carrier of glory, a vessel of revival.

Not long ago God gave us our littlest one yet at the time: a precious baby boy eight days old whose mother died from complications in childbirth. We were one of the only places around at the time who took in infants because of the extreme expense and extra work involved for the first two years. If we had not opened our arms to him, he would have had little chance of surviving his first year.

He did not have a name, so I had the amazing honor of naming him. He was one of the first babies I named. I looked into his small, sleeping, cherublike face and heard God tell me, *Daniel.*

This one will speak to governments, Jesus whispered in my ear. *He will rest in the midst of lions and not be touched. He will bring My word to kings.* Danieli, as he came to be called, was welcomed with great joy to our ever-growing family.

He was a statement from the heart of God, as all our babies have been, each in their own way. You have heard some of their stories: Ima, Benia, Azeezah. The nameless, faceless masses of the hurting, hungry and dying here in Sudan—each has a name. Each has a face, a calling and a destiny in the heart of God. Each one. Every one. The love of God gives names to the nameless and voices to the voiceless.

Danieli is now two years old. He still sports a scar on his chin where the medical personnel cut too close during his delivery. He runs around the compound like a small dirt magnet. He can manage three baths a day and still find more dirt. He is a little boy to the core. His great big grin lights up my day whenever he comes near.

I will never forget the first day he ran. I was standing under the partial shade of our rental compound's mango tree talking with a few of the mamas. I heard a little toddler's voice cry, "Mama! Mama!" I looked up just in time to see a small blue-clad missile running headlong as fast as his little legs would carry him over the uneven terrain. His arms were spread open wide. His gaze was fixed on mine. I almost wondered if he might leap and fly right into my arms. Instead he plowed into my leg and wrapped his chubby baby arms around me and looked up at me with a huge smile of satisfaction.

"Mama." He lifted his arms and waited until I knelt in the dirt to take him in my arms. Danieli. My Danny-boy. A promise fulfilled. I picked him up and remembered revival does indeed have a name.

Beth, Kojo, Data, Asa, Victoria Joy, Noora, Simon. I am learning every day how love gives the dignity of identity and calls forth the destiny of the very ones I have at times looked away from.

Our children have become some of my greatest teachers on this journey into God's heart. They worship with such passion and such fervency that they draw heaven down to our little bit of earth. I am watching them be captured by God's love. They lay hands on each other and pray for healing or for grace for exams or for whatever they need. And God shows up! When I am tired or frustrated, they will come and pray for me.

A little child will lead us. Unpaved roads are not scary to them. They are simply an adventure waiting to be explored. They are revival.

On Earth as It Is in Heaven

My eyes fill with tears when I see my children praying in the dirt with their hands raised to heaven, hungry for more Jesus. And when they lead worship on an outreach even our surrounding community stands amazed at what God is doing in and through their lives.

One day we were preparing to participate in an outreach at Freedom Square, a large dust field with a small stage on one end where many drunken men hang out with automatic weapons. I never know what I might find there. I have encountered everyone from madmen in chains to beggars to an assortment of hopeless, dull-eyed youth.

At this particular event I was invited to preach. Our team set up its speakers and equipment and formed a human boundary around the electronics to protect them from being stolen. We had set up right next to the barbed wire fence surrounding the local prison situated just on the edge of Freedom Square. Its location struck me as a bit ironic. I peered into the prison's vacant courtyard. *Everyone must be inside escaping the heat*, I thought. The crowd began to grow around us and press on us until I could feel the barbs of the wire fence behind me snagging my clothes.

I believed God wanted me to share on the reality of the Kingdom and to pray for the sick. It was perhaps the shortest sermon I have ever preached. It was about His Kingdom coming
in power. Soon a crowd of over five hundred surrounded us as
we spoke about the truth of His Kingdom coming on earth as
it is in heaven.

"Is there sickness in heaven?"

"No!" my children echoed back. They had heard this message before.

"Is there hunger in heaven?"

"No!" Slowly some of the crowd began to chime in.

"Is there cancer in heaven?"

"No!"

"Is there corruption and fighting in heaven?"

"No!"

"So we want to join in the prayer of Jesus, that His will shall
be done on earth as it is in heaven."

We closed the preaching with an invitation: "Who wants the
Kingdom of heaven? Who wants to follow Jesus and live in the
reality of the Kingdom of heaven now?" Every single person I
could see wanted Him—every hand in the crowd went up.

We then asked who had sickness or physical problems they
would like Jesus to heal. About three hundred hands went up.
Our team prayed a simple prayer of healing:

> Jesus, we ask for Your Kingdom to come and Your will to be
> done on earth as it is in heaven. We command all sickness and
> infirmity to go in Your name. All pain must go in Your name.
> We break off any curses and assignments of the enemy. In Your
> name we pray. Amen.

We asked for a show of hands, and approximately 90 percent of the people were healed or saw a change in their bodies after the first prayer. That was pretty exciting.

We then invited any who wanted additional prayer to come forward. A tall, middle-aged man named Jacob (not his real name) limped forward with a wooden underarm crutch. His ankle was evidently broken, and he said he was in a lot of pain. I knelt in the dirt and took his ankle in my hands, thinking, *Okay, Papa, please come and demonstrate what this all looks like.*

Again I simply prayed the prayer of Jesus: "Papa, Your Kingdom come here now on earth as it is in heaven."

I asked the man to test it, and he gingerly attempted to put weight on it. No pain. I held his crutch that was almost as tall as I was while he continued to check it for improvement. His ankle was totally healed. He took his crutch and left walking through the crowd with a big smile on his face. The crowd clapped. Hurray for God!

Revival did indeed have a name. That afternoon it was Jacob.

Many think success is about huge "revival" meetings of hundreds of thousands. Big meetings are great, and they have their place. But my favorite revival stories are the ones like those of Jacob and Danieli. My favorite stories are of those people who were shown the face of Jesus simply because someone saw and stopped.

Love is learning the names of the nameless, seeing and stopping for the one in front of me until that person becomes so transformed by love that he or she will stop for the one in front of him or her. In this way perhaps a city, a region, a nation will be transformed by love, one life at a time.

I am reminded again and again here: Love has a face. Mine.

Snapshots of Home

Last week I returned from a trip back to the United States. As I bounced down the familiar dirt road from the airstrip listening to the updates and chatter from Eudita and John, I sighed. It was good to be home. I would never have thought an unpaved road in the African bush could be so inviting, so familiar. Once again cathedrals made of dirt and our mud hut metropolis surrounded me. *Jesus, please keep building Your castle in my clay.*

As we pulled onto the compound our children lined the drive singing, "You are welcome today, our Mama in Jesus. Hallelujah in Jesus! You are welcome in Jesus. Hallelujah in Jesus!"

I hugged the children and greeted the staff, then I unlocked my room. The spiders had moved in and taken up residence in my absence. I have since engaged in a weeklong battle to evict my unwelcome houseguests. And it has taken almost as long to excavate the surfaces of my room from the dirt that engulfed them. It does not take long here for the sands of time to accumulate.

In a period of about thirty hours I went from running water, electricity and Starbucks back to my plastic jerry can and kerosene stove. It was a little jarring to my equilibrium. My transition back has been a bit bumpy this time, but unpaved roads have bumps.

I do love slums and leper colonies, but I also like my hot baths and cappuccinos. It would be less than honest if I told you that I love every aspect of living in the bush. I would not want you to think I am some super-saint with a Wonder Woman costume hidden in my closet. I do miss certain things. I would not be human if I did not. I am an ordinary person with ups and downs, highs and lows. I have good days and bad days. Some moments I want to pull out all my hair and become that barista I dream about. Sometimes I cannot fathom looking at another snotty nose or loving another person who is simply after our money.

I have moments of frustration. People came to introduce their "sister's children," but we soon found out that the children really belong to them; they just did not want to pay school fees anymore. It never ceases to amaze me how some people can lie to my face while looking me straight in the eye and smiling. I cannot even take a cookie without looking guilty.

Ultimately I am just a little woman who loves Jesus and longs to see and love as He does. For all the things I do not enjoy here, I have found many more that I do. The cost of convenience is a small price to pay in the big scheme of things. Look at what I have gained in return.

On my most recent trip to the United States, I printed a bunch of photos of the children. After reclaiming my room from dust and spiders, I began to put them up all over my crumbling walls. One afternoon Beth and some of my older girls joined me in my one-room home to hang out together. But our little gathering quickly turned into a crowd, as everyone wanted to see the pictures.

"Oh, look! There are Thomas and Davidi. I remember that day!"

"There are Noella and Noora—aren't they pretty? They have grown since those were taken."

Something special happens when someone loves you enough to put your photo on his or her wall or refrigerator. You feel a little more connected. You feel a little more like family. The chatter went on long into the evening. Somehow my children saw their photos on my wall and realized a little more that they belonged. This was their family and their home.

The children became just as excited to see one another's faces smiling back from my walls as they did their own. It is a beautiful thing to see them loving and preferring one another. I watched His love seep deeper into their hearts. Their eyes sparkled a little more than before. Looking into their eyes, my heart began to fill with His love. I am proud of them. And I would not trade a lifetime of hot baths for the opportunity to see God's dreams come to pass in each of their lives. That afternoon put things back into perspective.

I will always face difficulties and challenges. There is a cost. But the things that are most valuable are worth the expenditure when I allow Jesus to give me His eyes of love.

Called to Compassion

In this inside-out Kingdom, what is my response to a world in need all around me? What is my response to poverty, genocide, child trafficking and the global issues of oppression? Will I become so overwhelmed that I simply turn away? Believe me, I am tempted at times. But God has called me to His heart of compassion.

In September 2005 Sudan first crossed the radar screen of my awareness. I was sitting at my kitchen table in Colorado Springs not too long after I had initially heard Rolland Baker speak. I was channel surfing when a special on the children of Darfur caught my eye.

The image on the screen showed a Western woman sitting in the dirt surrounded by little dark African children covered in red dust. She was showcasing their crayon sketches of Kalashnikovs and the weapons of war that some were trying to deny existed. I heard their stories. I saw the pictures of their dreams. One little girl had drawn books because she wanted her brother to be able to go to school. A little boy drew his family being ripped apart as they ran from the birds that shot fire at them.

Before I knew it, the special was over and I was still sitting there weeping. A flood of compassion was released into my heart. My first call to Sudan was compassion. Thirteen months later I was living here.

The heart of God beats with this compassion that compelled me to action. If I truly see those who need help, then I will stop and ask what Jesus wants me to do. It might mean a short walk across the street. Or it might mean a journey around the world. But whatever it means to be the face of love as we each embrace our own unpaved road, true compassion begins in the heart of God.

Just before I moved to Africa in 2006, I was packing up my apartment in Colorado one evening when I started hearing audible music. I thought that was fairly odd because I did not have the CD player on. But it became louder. It had no words, just tone woven effortlessly upon tone. I had never heard anything like it.

I followed the sound to my sitting room and walked directly into a wall of God's presence. I lay down with my face on the floor. The sound grew louder and stronger, tone and sound woven with color and light, all-enveloping. I was being taken into an encounter with the compassionate heart of my Papa in heaven.

I began to hear the sounds of many children echoing in and out. Suddenly I was standing with Jesus in a vision surrounded by thousands and thousands of brown and black children. I just stood there and cried as I listened to them call me Mama. I was overwhelmed and thought, *Hmm, God, I am just one person and there are a lot of children here. I do not really do kids anymore. Why are they calling me Mama? There are so many of them!* I just stood there beset by a sea of brown and black faces, at a complete loss as to what to do next. Before I could go any further Jesus said, "Beloved, Father wants you."

Instantly (heaven has no time between thought and action) I was before the Father. I was looking into His chest, which was a burning, flaming, pulsing ball of fire. It looked like a million exploding stars, a nuclear reaction that was ebbing and flowing in rhythm like a cosmic visualization of the sound of the song I was hearing.

All I could think was, *What?*

Papa replied, "This is My heart."

I felt myself moving through His chest closer and closer to this flaming explosion of love. It drew me into it like a magnetic pull. Suspended in this mass of liquid love and fire, I felt no gravity, no bearing, no weight, no up, no down, no before, no after, no beginning, no end, nothing but eternity's now. Time ceased to hold any relevance.

I began to realize that this was the heart of compassion He wanted to put in me to carry. Not only did He want to immerse me in His heart of love, but He also wanted its burning, pulsating, eternal song to resonate in my own heart. This was the Father's blessing. This was the Father's song. And in the Father's heart I had truly come home.

Suddenly I was walking among the children again—thousands and thousands of them. They were crying, "Mama, Mama!" But this time I was not overwhelmed as I was before. Their cries made the flame of His love burn all the hotter inside of me until it began to burst forth from within my heart. One by one the children caught the flame and began themselves to burn and to run into the darkness to carry forth His light.

They sang the song I had heard in His heart, and as they burned with the fire of His love the night around them began to shine like day. Darkness and light became the same because the children carried His glory light within them, and heaven was more real to them than earth. Because of love they were fearless and unstoppable.

Compassion is not a weak word. It is the fiery reality of the Father's heart that compelled Him to give us His best in Jesus. It is the motivation of His inside-out Kingdom. It is the Good News of His love in action. It is the one word that easily could change our world if we would let it.

A Movement of Love

I found out the other day that southern Sudan alone has over a million orphans. That is a pretty staggering number. The whole of Sudan has three times that. My heart longs to see every one of them have a loving home. One person can do only so much. But what could one person loving one person who loves one person do? Our little group certainly cannot do everything. But each one of us can do something.

In the face of such devastating need I have wondered: What if a thousand people here simply took ten children into their homes, churches or villages? That number of a million orphans would be reduced by ten thousand right there. Ten thousand children would have homes simply because a company of people chose to see the needs around them through eyes of love and allow their responses to be compelled by heaven's compassion. A good plan and a well-funded program are not enough to meet the needs here. But a movement of love just might be.

What would a movement of love look like?

Could an army be raised up to fight hate with love, injustice with mercy, war with peace, poverty with generosity, despair with joy, striving with rest and religion with freedom? Can you imagine such an army?

The soldiers in this army would be fearless lovers of God. They would know His heart so well that they would carry His heartbeat everywhere they go. This Company of the Consumed would dream bigger than the pages of history and refuse to settle for what their eyes have seen. They would dance through the harvest fields of the nations with their gazes locked on the eyes of Love Himself.

His glory will cover the earth as waters cover the seas. We have His promise on that one (see Habakkuk 2:14). A movement of transformational love is rising up to be released from every tribe and tongue and nation. Those who wield this most powerful weapon called love are arising from the hidden and unseen depths of His heartbeat.

Have you seen them? The dangerous, fearless lovers of the King, who has so captured their gazes that no circumstance can distract them, no obstacle deter them.

They are the unlikely ones, the burning ones, the passionate ones whom the world has overlooked and called foolish. They will arise from the ends of the earth with a yes cry in their hearts and a song sung with their lives. Some of them are three, four and five years old and live in my house. But many more are waiting to be found.

What would a people look like who are fully embraced by love? What would a people become if they were totally set free to live out their own identity and sound? What would an army of love be, released from the darkest corners of the nations to carry the light of His face, seen through their own, as they see who they are in Love's eyes?

The wave dancers and light carriers are being released. The unpaved road is an invitation to the depths of Love's heartbeat. Watch out. Here they come: the unstoppable lovers of God whom nothing can deter. They bring with them life in abundance, light so bright that the darkness flees before its coming and night becomes as day at the rising of His glory in and through their lives.

The Edge of the Map

In the first chapter of this book I told you that life does not always lend itself to roadmaps. Now you have seen a little more what that has meant for me. Following the pursuit of God's heart has literally taken me off road and off the map. I have been to places in the last year that only Jesus and a few other people know exist—villages that are likely on no map anywhere in existence.

But they are not forgotten. God knows each hair on the elderly village grandmas' heads there. He knows the names of their grandbabies who joined the statistical ranks of the one in two children who die before they reach age five. He knows the names of the nameless, and no one is ever faceless to Him.

It has been a privilege to share with you my journey of discovering more of what it means to live loved by God and become an expression of His love to the people around me. The unpaved road into God's dreams has been quite the adventure. And I certainly have not arrived. I still have many miles left to explore, many chapters of this story left to live. Every day I learn a little more. Every day the adventure continues.

I could not have anticipated where this journey would take me in such a short time. Our family is less than three years old, and already God has done so much. Papa really has made His home with us just as He promised He would. I am humbled every day by His faithfulness.

As I look out at the coming of yet another year of His promises, I can scarcely fathom where the pursuit of His heart will take us in the days to come. Much that lies ahead of us here appears unstable and uncertain in the natural. But we live in the supernatural reality of His goodness where any storms that come are actually heaven's invitation to dance.

But what about you? In the beginning I told you I wanted you to keep reading right to the edge of the map—and then step off the known path into your own story lived from the center of His love.

Each of our paths will lead someplace unique. You may not be called to the bush of Africa to love forgotten children (or you might be!). But as each of us embraces our individual unpaved road into His heart of love, as each of us encounters more what it means to be the face of His love in places of pain around us, truly His Kingdom comes.

I want to invite you to a life lived beyond the edge of the map.

At the edge of the map, a holy adventure awaits. A movement of love is arising in those who will choose to lay down their lives each day, becoming the expression of God's grace and goodness to the people He brings them. Heaven is becoming so real to this coming generation that earth will begin to fade into a shadow.

We are invited to join a global tribe of sons and daughters of their Father in heaven whose silence is louder than the shouts of multitudes, whose prayers are stronger than the decrees of kings, whose authority is found in humility, whose gaze is fixed on eternity, whose lives are found in giving them away. We are called to be part of the coming of an upside-down, inside-out Kingdom where the last are first and the greatest are servants of all.

At the edge of the map is a company of those who are emerging from garbage heaps and refugee camps, from universities and shopping malls—those found in unexpected places at unlikely times, called from far-flung corners of the earth to converge in God's heart for such a time as this. Here we are the desperate ones. We eat the bread of hunger. We drink the cup of longing. We choose to look beyond what appears to be to what really is. The world has written many of us off, left us for dead, pushed us aside and rendered us invisible. But heaven has heard our cries, caught our tears and whispered our destinies into visions at night that dance across our sleep and wake us with their songs.

And now heaven calls us forth to make real God's unformed dreams in this hour until the essence of His beauty crowns the ash heaps of nations and the dawning of His glory chases away even the memory of darkness. The world may never know our names, never see our faces; but heaven hears our cries. And on this unpaved journey into the heart of our King we are called to become the whisper of His hope, the voice of His truth and the face of His love.

Eternity has written its story on our hearts. We have only one life to give, so we give it away extravagantly, hilariously, without reserve. We could not imagine we'd get to pour out our lives loving Him and seeing His eyes find us again and again in the gaze of broken, hurting humanity.

We are not those content to bloom in greenhouses and gardens alone. Our hearts long for the wastelands and war zones of our day. Our roots are firmly anchored in heaven, and from there our wings are released to soar on the earth. Our no's have been burned away in the fire of God's love. Only a yes-cry lived out with our lives moment by moment remains.

This is life lived beyond the edge of the map. God's heart of love is calling you. Nations are waiting for your yes to His unpaved road. Are you ready?

Papa, I want to thank You for the ones reading these words.

I ask right now, Holy Spirit, that You wash over them and fill them with Your perfect love. Give them child-eyes to see the invitation of the unpaved road. Draw them deeper into Your heart, that they may live all of life from the place of knowing how loved they are. Papa, wrap Your arms around them. Let them hear the songs You sing over them in the night. Let them know the place they have in Your house. Let them know that You love them because you love them.

I ask You, Papa, to stir hunger in them and call forth the dreams You have placed in their hearts that they have not even dared to embrace. Take them lower in humility, deeper in intimacy and higher in revelation. I ask that You submerge them in Your fiery presence until they are see-through in love and carry Your glory wherever they go.

I ask You for a movement of love to begin one life at a time that will literally change nations from the inside out. Teach all of us how to dance in the storm, and let us live a life of love without limit. Amen.

Michele Perry is actively involved in mobilizing a movement of those called to live in love and carry God's light into the darkest and hardest places on earth. For more than fifteen years she has ministered and spoken around the world. Her ministry is characterized by supernatural displays of love where the manifest presence of God comes with power. She is ordained and sent out by Heidi and Rolland Baker and Iris Ministries, Inc.

Michele is the pioneering director for Iris Ministries Sudan, founded in 2006. She also founded Converge International in 2007 to connect like-hearted individuals, organizations and gatherings with the front lines of transformation in the nations.

She loves the least, the unlikely and the unexpected. She will go anywhere anytime to see the dreams of Jesus fulfilled.

Michele travels regularly internationally and is available to speak at churches, conferences, community gatherings, universities and wherever people are hungry for more than they can currently see.

You may contact Michele with comments or questions at irisminsudan@gmail.com

For more information please see the following websites:

Michele's blog: lovehasaface.blogspot.com
Michele's personal website: www.changethewayyousee.org
Iris Ministries Sudan: www.iris-sudan.org
Converge International: www.convergeinternational.net